Nursery Nurse to Early Years' Practitioner

The role, relationships and responsibilities of the traditional 'nursery nurse' have changed markedly within the last 20 years, demanding a high level of skill, knowledge, and understanding which pertains to formal international standards. This book responds to the needs of a workforce who have experienced rapid developments and challenges. It supports an understanding of 'self' and the creation of an organisational pedagogy.

Concepts are explored by reference to research indicating the importance of relationship-based practice with children and parents. Experienced practitioner Hazel Whitters draws on practical examples from the field, such as attachment, inclusion, pedagogy and child protection to bridge the implementation gap between current research, policy and practice of work in the early years.

Nursery Nurse to Early Years' Practitioner will be of interest to early years' practitioners, academics, post-graduate students, researchers and course leaders in the field.

Hazel G. Whitters is a senior early years' worker and child protection coordinator in a voluntary organisation in Glasgow. She has conducted research in child protection and early intervention.

Nursery Nurse to Early Years' Practitioner
Role, Relationships and Responsibilities

Hazel G. Whitters

LONDON AND NEW YORK

First published 2017
by Routledge
2 Park Square, Milton Park, Abingdon, Oxon OX14 4RN

and by Routledge
711 Third Avenue, New York, NY 10017

Routledge is an imprint of the Taylor & Francis Group, an informa business

© 2017 Hazel G. Whitters

The right of Hazel G. Whitters to be identified as author of this work has been asserted by her in accordance with sections 77 and 78 of the Copyright, Designs and Patents Act 1988.

All rights reserved. No part of this book may be reprinted or reproduced or utilised in any form or by any electronic, mechanical, or other means, now known or hereafter invented, including photocopying and recording, or in any information storage or retrieval system, without permission in writing from the publishers.

Trademark notice: Product or corporate names may be trademarks or registered trademarks, and are used only for identification and explanation without intent to infringe.

British Library Cataloguing-in-Publication Data
A catalogue record for this book is available from the British Library

Library of Congress Cataloging-in-Publication Data
A catalog record for this book has been requested

ISBN: 978-1-138-07103-2 (hbk)
ISBN: 978-1-315-11483-5 (ebk)

Typeset in Times New Roman
by Apex CoVantage, LLC

I dedicate this book to the staff, parents, carers and children of the Jeely Piece Club in Castlemilk, Glasgow; to the academic and library staff of the University of Strathclyde; and finally to my husband, John.

Your knowledge and insight inspired me to write this book and gave me deep understanding to share with others. Thank you.

Contents

	Introduction	1
1	Nursery nurse to early years' practitioner	7
2	Keyworker and child relationship	25
3	Child protection in the early years	49
4	Pedagogy and the implementation gap	73
	Index	*89*

Introduction

The role, relationships, and responsibilities of the traditional nursery nurse have changed markedly within the last five to 20 years, and they demand a high level of skill, knowledge, and understanding which pertain to formal international standards. The early years' worker in the twenty-first century is a registered professional whose expertise is sought within integrated teams of health, education and social work, children's panel, and court. The traditional role of the nursery nurse has been transformed, and the early years' practitioner is an educator, carer, attachment figure, pedagogue, counsellor, and safe-guarder whose work has an impact value which lasts a lifetime. The sector tends to attract long-term vocational workers, and this book responds to the needs of a workforce who have experienced rapid developments and challenges.

Several factors have contributed to this re-focus upon the earliest years of childhood. Research in the field of neuroscience has publicised the significance of sensitive periods for development from pre-birth to 3 years of age (National Scientific Council on the Developing Child, 2016). Adversity in childhood has been linked to a propensity to mental health issues, crime, and under-achievement in education (Sroufe, Egeland, Carlson & Collins, 2006). The media has associated limitations upon brain development with poverty and inequality in society, and growing public awareness has led to a demand for an increase in learning opportunities for young children. The concept of a working parent has become familiar in communities and has resulted in extended day care for children. Recently, government funding in the UK has been diverted from reactive intervention in the teenage years to preventative strategies in the early years.

The role of keyworker as an attachment figure who creates a base for learning, originally promoted in 1985, has great significance in the current day care of children (Goldschmied & Jackson, 1985). Professionals have gained knowledge and understanding of early brain development, and workers are familiar with the effects of secure and insecure attachment

2   *Introduction*

throughout a lifespan. Promotion of equality and inclusion and supporting the next generation to be educated, effective contributors have led to changes in legislation and guidance. Practice has evolved, and many children with long- or short-term additional support needs attend mainstream early years' services as opposed to specialist units.

High-profile cases have provided realistic illustration of society's responsibility to safeguard children, and professional understanding of child protection has been extended to encompass the promotion of resilience to adversity, and support to achieve potential. The attainment gap and inclusion agenda were formerly topics associated with primary and secondary schools, but research has linked achievement with the pre-birth to 5-year-old period; this philosophy has had a significant impact on the requirements of early years' workers. Previously termed *desirable* skills have been recategorised as *essential* for employment in the sector.

Training providers can rapidly respond to these needs for undergraduate students; however, continuous professional development for qualified employed workers is not so readily available or accessible. An example is the Working with Under Threes course which was delivered sporadically to the workforce in the 1980s and 1990s following the research of Elinor Goldschmied. This course incorporated the role of keyworker and specific activities for the younger age group which included the use of the Treasure Basket and Heuristic Play. These aspects of play have become an integral component of current training courses, but I continue to encounter groups of long-standing practitioners who have 'missed' this opportunity for continuous professional development. Additionally, many aspects of early years' work which are taught in the pre-qualification and pre-employment period need to be reviewed with the expertise and maturity of practice in the field. The passing of time and practical skill support a deeper understanding of concepts and theories which contributes to development of practice.

This book focuses upon the changing role, relationships, and responsibilities of the workforce within the early years. The reader is supported to develop practice through an increase in knowledge and, subsequently, understanding of approaches and aspects of care and education which have been introduced over the last five to 20 years. For example:

- A therapeutic relationship with children and parents as a secure base for learning
- Therapeutic play
- Learning opportunities which promote inclusion and respond to complex needs of children
- Partnership-working within an integrated team
- Preventative intervention as a contribution to child protection

- Child-led pedagogy
- Individual and collective responsibility and accountability
- The use of legislation, generic guidance, and cultural sensitivity as features which contribute to closing the 'implementation gap'

Changes in the early years have occurred iteratively, and continuous professional development is dependent on funding/opportunities from an employer or the motivation of the individual to seek out learning. In-service training tends to focus upon issues associated with legislation and curriculum, and this book responds to a need for information which directly affects practice by reflecting current research.

I highlight the dichotomy of personal and of professional beliefs and the link to attitude and to behaviour. Legislation publicises optimum outcomes in the context of national or international frameworks. Guidance is generic and delivers information for practitioners to interpret and apply within an organisation. I describe the impact upon practitioners as guidance that is transferred into legislation is linked to professional responsibility and accountability.

This book aims to empower practitioners to recognise current skills and professional potential, to identify a unique organisational pedagogy, to implement intervention with cultural sensitivity, and to complement the strengths of their colleagues within integrated teams. An understanding of 'self' in a professional context is a necessary base for seeking out comprehension of policy in order to enhance practice in each organisation.

Early years' workers will be supported to use their knowledge and expertise and to value their skills and personalities which can be applied in creating effective keyworker-to-child, practitioner-to-parent, and professional-to-professional relationships. Frequent examples of practice are given throughout the text to make knowledge accessible to practitioners in the context of daily work. Terms which are applicable to the field are applied and explained throughout the book.

I have practised and studied for over 30 years in the field of child care and education within a variety of settings – for example, learning in the earliest years (pre-birth to 5), primary schools (5 to 12), residential care, and emergency respite. Each setting has a common context of professionals as service-providers and of families as service-users. Daily transitions from home to settings provide opportunities for parents and professionals to share, collaborate, and forge a plan of support. Goals are generally universal – achievement of potential, development, success.

My experiences have taught me the importance of seeking and sharing knowledge, educating and being educated, accepting and questioning, respecting and responding: team skills in the partnerships. Legislation directs practice, but learning which leads to development of children and parents occurs through local implementation of statutes within an organisation and in the context of a community. My understanding and skills have evolved over many years of practising, reflecting upon mistakes and successes, and observing and seeking out explanation. I am indebted to countless parents and children, in addition to numerous colleagues who have responded to my quest for knowledge.

Research indicates the importance of relationship-based practice. The significance of the parent-professional relationship has been publicised for the last 60 years. As students we are given frameworks of the optimum skills to use in forging relationships with parents. We learn about 'hostile and disaffected families,' which includes protection of the worker, physically and emotionally. We are warned to be aware of professional versus personal opinions. We strive to identify the boundary of friendship and professionalism. We are taught that a demonstration of empathy will support the achievement of an optimum parent-professional relationship, which is often termed the therapeutic alliance. Equal partnerships with parents are promoted as desirable outcomes from policy which are linked to a child's achievement of potential.

Services have been challenged and ultimately enhanced by *new approaches* in the last two decades which focus upon preventative work. The key to effective implementation is the promotion of knowledge and understanding at strategic and operational level, in addition to updating the general public. The optimum care of children and their families encapsulates pedagogy which regards each child as an individual – a unique human being whose interpretation and perception of his or her world is paramount to the responsive care by professionals and parents.

Chapter 1 – 'Nursery nurse to early years' practitioner' – describes the change in role of the traditional nursery nurse from the 1800s to current day. Findings from research, an increase in day care for children under 5 years of age, implementation of a formal curriculum, and mandatory qualifications are issues which have shaped the responsibilities of early years' practitioners in settings. The chapter gives a description of therapeutic play and uses theory of attachment to support the reader's comprehension of this approach to learning for children in their earliest years.

Chapter 2 – 'Keyworker and child relationship' – explains the importance of a secure attachment relationship between the keyworker and child in a context of current research in neuroscience, theory, and the link to practice. The chapter uses many common examples from practice to complement the presentation of theoretical frameworks and to enable readers to gain a deep understanding of actions, purpose, and outcomes for the service-users. The minutiae of playroom sessions are highlighted and given significance by linking research to development in children under 3 years of age and relationships throughout a lifespan.

Chapter 3 – 'Child protection in the early years'– focuses upon the use of relationship-based practice and accesses theory to promote comprehension of child protection. The chapter discusses the change in child protection over the last 20 years which has led to pre-crisis intervention and supporting children's resilience to adversities. Felt, expressed, and normative needs are defined and described through examples. Differences and similarities in the perceptions of parents and professionals are reviewed within a context of research and daily practice.

Chapter 4 – 'Pedagogy and the implementation gap' – describes a weakness in the links between research and practice in the workplace. Sources of knowledge, use of reflective practice, and peer support for professional development are discussed. The emotional impact of child protection upon the practitioner is described, and suggestions are made for practical responses. The chapter promotes strategies for recording and disseminating observations and assessments within a playroom team, a service team, and an integrated team of multi-disciplinary professionals. Pedagogy is explored, as is the approach to identifying and promoting an organisational pedagogy which reflects the principles of each service. Key messages conclude this chapter.

References

National Scientific Council on the Developing Child. (2016). *The science of early childhood development: closing the gap between what we know and what we do.* Cambridge: Harvard University.

Sroufe, L. A., Egeland, B., Carlson, E., & Collins, W. A. (2006). Placing early attachment experiences in developmental context. In K. E. Grossman, K. Grossman & E. Watters (Eds.), *Attachment from infancy to adulthood: the major longitudinal studies* (pp. 48–70). New York: The Guilford Press.

Goldschmied, E., & Jackson, S. (1985). *People under three-young children in day care.* London: Routledge.

1 Nursery nurse to early years' practitioner

This chapter looks at the changing role, relationships, and responsibilities of the worker in a context of early years. The chapter describes the development of care to include education and the development of education to encompass the therapeutic relationship and attachment with a primary or secondary carer: parent or professional. The change in identity from solitary practitioner to a worker within an extended integrated team is explored, and the impact of registration upon practice, accountability, and responsibility is discussed. The changes in comprehension of different types of play (including therapeutic play) and the links to pedagogy are explained through reference to research. The topics of cultural sensitivity and of implementation of the curriculum within each organisation are introduced in this chapter and further explored throughout the book.

Nursery nurse

Two hundred years ago, nursery nurses traditionally cared for children in a family home, hospital, or institutions which supported children who would be currently termed as vulnerable due to additional support needs. The role was primarily provision of physical and social care and of elementary education. Emotional care was a concept which was prominent in the 1800s by association with child development. During the nineteenth century, researchers and theorists sought understanding of the concept of learning and of development during childhood years. It is clear that there are differences and similarities between the philosophies of past educators and current significance, which is given to aspects of learning. Froebel, in the early 1800s, had identified a correlation between learning, a mother's love, play, and the input from trained educators. Macmillan, in the latter part of the 1800s, emphasised the importance of holistic development by focusing upon a child's physical, educational, and emotional needs. Rudolph Steiner promoted children's individuality and expressed that education and mental wellbeing were achieved through a balance of skills, knowledge, and the human spirit. Comprehension of education and care in the 1900s was influenced by Montessori teaching the importance of the intellect being led by the five senses. Additionally, at this time, Vygotsky included social interaction with adults and peers as necessary to cognition, and Piaget identified that each child's interpretation and comprehension of the environment related to knowledge acquisition and, ultimately, to development. Bowlby presented the basis for learning as emotional in the form of a secure relationship with an attachment figure (Macleod-Brudenell, Cortvriend, Hallet, Kay & Walkup, 2004).

Education and care of children were promoted by the use of different approaches – for example, the American High-Scope programme which commenced in the 1960s supported children to learn by planning, exploring through play, and reflecting upon outcomes and potential future goals. These strategies from High-Scope were adopted within UK nurseries in the 1980s and followed the mandate of 'Plan (Think), Play (Do), and Put Away (Reflect).' The Reggio Emilia approach was developed in Italy and placed emphasis on the self-worth of individuals by supporting each child to recognise skills and talents. These principles were also applied within the UK and based upon the premise that high self-esteem enables the learning process to take place with optimum value for the child. The Plowden Report (Central Advisory Council for Education, 1967) recommended a child-centred curriculum which reflected the needs of each child in addition to *whole class teaching*. New Zealand's Te Whariki considered the importance of influences from family and local community upon learning, and these principles are reflected in National Practice Models (Department for Children, Schools and Families, 2009; Scottish Government, 2008).

The curricula and practice models which are applied in services in the UK today have been influenced by these aspects of learning from past educators in the field of child development. The main themes which have been established as important to learning in the early years are emotional wellbeing, play, support by practitioners and parents, a holistic approach, environment, and an outcome of educated, caring citizens.

Towards the end of the twentieth century, there was a growing realisation from researchers and educators that the period from birth to 5 years of age, or pre-school stage, required a specific approach to provision of learning opportunities rather than 'watered down school activities,' as frequently expressed by early years' practitioners. By this time many establishments were providing day care for children in the birth to 3-year age group in the form of parent-toddler groups, play-groups, and local authority day care in nurseries for the most vulnerable children. Organisations had started to create local curricula for the youngest children in their care, and, at the turn of the twenty-first century in the UK, a national curriculum was disseminated to the early years' workforce. In the UK context, the first curriculum framework for pre-school children was published in 1999 – A Curriculum Framework 3 to 5 Years (Scottish Executive, 1999). The Early Years' Foundation Stage (Department for Education and Skills, 2000) was published soon after and followed by the Welsh Foundation Stage, 3–7 (Welsh Assembly Government, 2004), and the Curriculum for Excellence, 3–18 (Scottish Executive, 2004). Birth to Three Matters (Surestart, 2002), Birth to Three: Supporting Our Youngest Children (Scottish Executive, 2005), and Pre-Birth to Three: Positive Outcomes for Scotland's Children and Families (Scottish Government, 2010) are curricula with a focus upon children in the pre-3-year stage of development. Getting It Right for Every Child (Scottish Government, 2008) and the Common Assessment Framework (Department for Children, Schools and Families, 2009) are national practice models to support assessment of needs and delivery of the curriculum.

The term 'nursery nurse' began to be replaced in order to reflect the changing responsibilities of the early years' practitioner: educator, carer, communicator, and safe-guarder. Common role names which remain in use within the UK include child development officer (local authority), pre-five worker, early years' practitioner, early years' development worker, and, more recently, pedagogue.

Emotional wellbeing and play

The *Concise Oxford Dictionary* defines **well-being** as the state of feeling comfortable and happy – thus linking physical and emotional status. **Play** is defined as engaging in games or other activities for enjoyment rather than serious or practical purpose (Oxford University Press, 1999). It is difficult to present a universal definition of play which is relevant to today's children. The concept of play is equated with learning; therefore, it relates to a child's interaction and involvement with the environment. The **setting in which play occurs** has a direct or indirect impact upon the child's exploration through the promotion of boundaries: natural or human-made environmental parameters, behavioural boundaries, the expectation of an outcome, or emotional boundaries created by the relationship and interaction with an adult or peer. The **effect of play** can be understood by the main attributes as demonstrated by the child – for example, physical play encompassing gross and fine motor skills; intellectual play focusing upon linguistic, scientific, mathematical, and creative learning; and social and emotional play which includes therapeutic interaction (Moyles, 1989). There is a current tendency to categorise play by the principles which relate to the pedagogy of an organisation – for example, adult-led, child-centred, or child-led. Research (Siraj-Blatchford et al., 2003) has indicated that the richest environment for child development includes a range of **opportunities for play** in a variety of settings with the support of an attachment figure.

Children's needs and interests can change rapidly. A responsive practitioner observes a child, recognises implicit and explicit cues, evaluates in relation to the child's current and past circumstances, and uses her or his skills and knowledge to implement practice. Each child should be offered care and education which responds directly to need in a timely manner. This approach may involve changes to the environment, adult intervention or withdrawal, and emotional support. An aim is to increase involvement and wellbeing of every child due to the correlation between learning and emotional status. The outcome is to include and to integrate every child into the early years' learning environment. Pedagogy should reflect individuality of children, and the approach should be understood by all practitioners, students, seniors, management, and parents within a setting. For example, child-led pedagogy encompasses environmental, social, and emotional boundaries as described previously, and practice can be affected if this aspect is unclear to workers, children, or parents.

Ferre Laevers (1994) created the Leuven Involvement Scale, which is increasingly popular throughout the UK as a tool which supports practitioners to gain an understanding of the link between emotional wellbeing and learning for each child. The child is observed for a short period and assessed in relation to five stages of involvement and five stages of emotional wellbeing; thereafter, the results are evaluated and contribute to the formation of a care plan. Good practice entails practitioners being supported by their team to interpret the scales and to identify contributory factors to the child's involvement/wellbeing. The team have a responsibility to implement strategies which support the child to develop. The following aspects relate to interpretation of the five stages from the Leuven Scale within a practice context of early years.

Child involvement

1 *The child may observe the environment without involvement or create a barrier between himself or herself and setting – for example, by covering his or her eyes or turning towards the carer.*
2 *The child's involvement is easily interrupted by an external factor which stops the child's interaction.*

3 The child's involvement does not have a focus, and the child is easily distracted but can resume the activity.
4 The child appears to have a plan and focus for involvement in play. The child is able to concentrate on the activity for short periods.
5 Fully engaged in meaningful play – the child demonstrates that he or she is following his or her interests, creating and implementing a plan, and responding to his or her needs.

Child wellbeing

1 The child shows clear signals of distress and may attempt to leave the environment or seek support from the carer.
2 The child may observe but not interact with the environment. Facial expression and neutral posture show little or no emotion.
3 Facial expression and posture demonstrate that the child is beginning to relax and feels comfortable to interact within the environment.
4 The child demonstrates obvious signs of self-confidence and enjoyment in play.
5 The child demonstrates obvious signs of self-confidence and high self-esteem.

If emotional wellbeing is a requisite for play, then play is confirmation of a child's emotional wellbeing. The concept of play has developed over the last two centuries from a leisure activity directed by children on an ad hoc basis, with limited adult intervention, to structured play used by adults as a teaching method. Planned structured group play was used as a teaching medium within the early years from the 1960s to the 1990s. Each nursery nurse planned and presented an activity, to a key group of children, which had defined learning outcomes relating to developmental checklists. This behaviourist approach created an environment in which the child was integrated into the society of the playroom but not necessarily included. Thomas and Loxley (2001) describe inclusion as the assimilation of children (with additional needs) into a mainstream setting which involves comprehensive education, equality, and collective belonging. Integration entails the children adapting to the status quo in order to conform.

Edmunds and Stewart-Brown (2003) made the distinction between socially competent, socially desirable, and socially conformist behaviour. Children who experience structured activities learn social and emotional competence by achieving socially desirable and conformist behaviour. Social and emotional competence may promote emotional wellbeing but only within an identified setting. Edmunds and Stewart-Brown suggested that this behaviour may be counter-productive in terms of nurturing desirable attitudes for long-term gain, such as positive mental health and good citizenship. This type of approach results in the child being reliant on the adult to regulate his or her behaviour. Additionally, the child's ability to demonstrate socially acceptable behaviour, within a breadth of settings, is dependent on his or her capacity to transfer learned social conformity between settings.

Concepts are granted prominence in relation to research, and this may create a philosophy which can lead to national recognition in the form of curricula or teaching practices. Society's attitude to a concept often changes when ideas become enshrined in legislation or formal publications. The Effective Provision of Pre-school Education 1997–2003 identifies elements of effective pedagogy as being the level and type of interactions between adults, children, and the environment (Siraj-Blatchford et al., 2003). Play is promoted as the interface between the elements, and the adult and child's sustained shared thinking is the main catalyst. The findings from this research project have had a significant impact upon the pedagogy in early years' establishments.

Today, play in early years' settings is primarily associated with child-led active learning which is directed by a child following his or her interests. Practitioners support the child to access and choose from a range of activities, and they extend the learning opportunities by acting as co-facilitators. Opportunities for participative and cooperative play allow children to learn the social rules of their micro-systems, including appropriate communication techniques and the formation of friendships. Symbolic and imaginative play enables children to make sense of their past experiences and associated emotions and to prepare for future events.

Bowlby (1979) described how the attachment process is a forum for young children to display their most intense emotions; therefore, the quality of attachment relationship greatly influences emotional wellbeing. Three directions of motivation in babies are identified by Trevarthan and Aitken (2001), as well as three corresponding functions of emotion which contribute positively or negatively to the fundamental organisation of a baby's learning. This research provided practitioners with an increase in comprehension of the rationale for sensory activities which had been introduced to the workforce many years previously – for example, Treasure Basket and Heuristic Play.

Treasure Basket and Heuristic Play

The Treasure Basket and Heuristic Play were introduced to nurseries in 1985 (Goldschmied & Jackson, 1985). The rationale was to support learning for children under 3 years of age by creating an environment and using supportive strategies which responded to emotional and intellectual needs.

These activities are designed to support children's comprehension of themselves – the child's inner working model. The Treasure Basket and Heuristic Play are examples of play being presented to children through a planned structured environment. The execution of the activity involves a child's active learning, and the adult relinquishes control of the situation as soon as the child enters the area; therefore, the power-base is given to the child. The adult's role is that of silent observer and attachment figure who portrays support and reassurance by positive body language. If ideas were to be promoted by an adult through verbal interaction, then it could lead the child's thoughts in a direction dictated by the adult perspective rather than the child's own interests and needs. Sensory activities facilitate children to learn by using their personal bases of knowledge and understanding which encompass their previous emotional and social experiences. Children focus upon their inner worlds as opposed to involvement with the environment which is stimulated by external interaction with adults or peers. The following information depicts examples from practice in early years' settings.

Treasure basket

The baby is usually aged between 6 and 12 months, and the experience may last for half an hour. The treasure basket consists of a round receptacle made of a natural material, usually a wicker basket, which contains approximately 20 natural objects suitable for exploration by a non-ambulant baby who is able to sit unsupported and to reach for toys. The round shape of the receptacle enables the baby to choose from a broad displayed selection of learning materials and to access objects easily and independently. One key adult figure sits in close proximity to the baby and presents positive body language in response to the baby's actions, an important feature of the secure attachment relationship. The surrounding environment facilitates the baby's sensory exploration and choice-making through minimisation of distractions and through promotion of an ambient atmosphere. For example, lighting should be adequate but not stimulating, the potential for external noise interference should be reduced, and floor covering should be comfortable for baby and carer.

The rationale of the Treasure Basket is to support the first and second level of development of a sense of self – as a physical and social being. The right side of a baby's brain is ready to learn at this stage through input from the five senses. The baby begins to demonstrate patterns of cause and effect through instinctive exploration – for example, noticing an object, stretching with one or perhaps two hands, maintaining sitting balance, touching, grasping, and eventually gaining knowledge and increased understanding of the object through exploration by hands or mouth. This action elevates the baby's basic level of understanding from initial observation to rich comprehension and memory of the object. Babies who are using treasure baskets also gain practice in spatial awareness of the learning environment and their own physical selves. At an elementary level, the babies are creating a plan and implementing it in relation to their own ideas – interacting, learning about, and interpreting their worlds – the babies are using their volition to explore their proximal environments of the Treasure Baskets. The baby learns that the presence of the key adult is necessary to his or her discoveries. An inquisitive baby will frequently refer to the adult by glancing or maintaining eye contact. This eye contact may be supplemented by the baby reaching forward to the adult in order to make physical contact. The baby is seeking and confirming the attachment status.

The original teaching of these activities took place in the 1980s and focused primarily upon the actions and behaviour of the attachment figure within the context of presenting the Treasure Basket or Heuristic Play activities. Comprehension of the benefit to the child and of the link between theory and practice was not widely communicated to practitioners in the field. Research was common in the topic of attachment and development at that time; however, the findings and knowledge were not readily available to practitioners. Since professional registration, and an increasing awareness of the significance of attachment to human beings, practitioners have been able to access the research which informs legislation and guidance. The knowledge base of early years' workers has been extended remarkably, and this aspect of professional development has improved practice.

It is essential that early years' practitioners are aware of the rationale of these examples and many other sensory activities for children in the youngest age group, so that the adult embraces the responsive role of attachment figure and understands the link to development in the earliest years. Research supports an increase in comprehension of the worker, and, subsequently, strategies can be adapted to meet the needs of individual children; good practice becomes reproducible and is consistently implemented by each practitioner and the whole team. Standards can be recognised and attained within an organisation which provides a necessary base for reflection upon the output of a service and areas for development.

Heuristic play

Heuristic play is presented to the ambulant child, usually about 12–20 months old, in a group of peers, and it may last for an hour. The presence of an adult provides a readily available attachment figure who represents a constant and consistent base for learning for each child. Most keyworkers have several children in their key group who are the appropriate age and stage for Heuristic Play; therefore, the number of adults in the area can be limited.

The rationale of Heuristic Play is to further support the child's understanding of self through self-directed exploration of a planned learning environment which incorporates opportunities for problem-solving. The third level of self encompasses a profound understanding of the concepts of cause and effect, and the fourth level is the ability and capacity to plan and implement ideas. Comprehension of cause and effect is the necessary basis for problem-solving, and it links to numeracy, literacy, physical achievement, and the creation of relationships. Putting a plan into action supports children to understand their impact upon the learning environment, and it has a positive effect on children's self-esteem and knowledge of their power-base. The left side of the young child's brain is ready for learning at this stage. Memories which are already stored in the right side of the brain, based upon previous sensory input, gain greater understanding for children as their language develops – termed **coherent narrative**.

Practitioners are taught to support children emotionally and physically by adopting this role of a secure attachment figure and by allowing all children to use their own interests to extend and consolidate their learning. Children become regulators and judges of their own skills, using their power to maintain or to change the learning environment. Fonagy (1999) notes that a strong attachment system regulates children's emotional experiences and wellbeing, leading to increased resilience. Fonagy, Gergely, and Target (2007) report on the importance of activating the link between the different aspects of self which, combined with attachment bonds, leads to physical and social development.

Heuristic Play is presented in the form of ten to 20 natural receptacles of different shapes and sizes placed on a comfortable floor area, within a quiet environment. Each container is filled with approximately 50 objects which are identical – for example, 50 tea strainers or 50 wooden spoons or 50 small rubber balls or 50 feathers. Receptacles should respond to potential schemas which children frequently demonstrate at this stage of development. **Schema** refers to recurrent behaviour of a child during interactions with his or her environment which form patterns – demonstrating repetition of movement and organisation by the child. For example, receptacles should provide opportunities for a child to participate in transporting; hiding; threading; building structures horizontally, vertically, or in a circular shape; gathering; enveloping; rotating; positioning; and repetitively carrying objects back and forward.

Children use schemas at the sensorimotor level as they develop understanding of their physical impact upon the world, and symbolically during imaginative play. Neural pathways are formed through repeating the same activities. Over time children may develop several schemas which they use independently or collectively to develop their ideas into a coordinated complex approach to learning. As with the Treasure Basket, the variety of objects should have the potential to stimulate the five senses.

The attachment figure supports the child throughout a session by positive reinforcement of the child's efforts, without judgement or qualification or extension. The adult sits on the floor with open body language, inclined towards the child's play space, and the adult may smile, touch the child briefly, or stroke the child gently – these are all techniques which early years' practitioners use to establish and reaffirm an attachment relationship. The adult is indicating: 'I care, I am with you, I support your efforts, I help you to recognise your achievements, I encourage you to be resilient, and you are the focus of my world at this point.' The presence of an attachment figure liberates a child to play, learn, and develop.

In the early stages of an attachment relationship, physical contact is required to promote the child's comprehension of the link to emotional wellbeing. During later stages, light or momentary physical touch or nurturing represents an established attachment relationship. Over time, the child can use the effect of the secure base for learning from an attachment relationship even if the adult is not present. The child's inner working model is forming and encompasses the memory of emotional wellbeing, actions, and behaviour which the child associates with the company of his or her attachment figure. Practitioners often comment that children will frequently use the name of their main carer during the settling period in early years' settings, and this auditory input stimulates a positive memory for a young child.

It used to be believed that reminding children of their carers during periods of separation (for example, hospital stays or day care) would trigger an adverse emotional reaction from the children. Current practice has developed from an increase in comprehension, and an effective technique to nurture attachment is to display large photographs of child and carer within the setting. The child is encouraged to refer to these photographs during times of emotional stress and emotional wellbeing. The use of mirrors and family or keyworker and child photographs support a child's understanding of self and present visual reminders of the child's relationships with primary and secondary carers.

The promotion of inclusion and equality has resulted in children with complex needs attending early years' settings as opposed to specialist services. This has changed the role of practitioners who require an increase in knowledge and expertise to respond effectively to each child's needs. Every child experiences short-term additional support needs, and many children will require long-term support throughout childhood. The additional support for learning needs in young children cannot be generalised or definitively categorised. Needs may relate to diagnosed disabilities, undiagnosed needs, and reaction to trauma. The UK and other countries in the world are nations of many cultures, and families may be distant from one another due to socio-economic, cultural, or personal issues. The source of trauma may never be identified for many children who are fleeing from war or persecution to seek solace in another country.

Therapeutic intervention

Therapeutic play – for example, the use of Treasure Basket, Heuristic Play, or relationship therapy (Bratton, Landreth, Kellam & Blackard, 2006) – can offer children who are growing up in adverse socio-economic or socio-emotional circumstances an opportunity to understand experiences and emotions, to develop self-control and responsibility, and ultimately to build resilience.

Erikson (1999) expresses that play provides a self-healing mechanism for children. Interventions often focus upon the creation of a secure attachment relationship with a practitioner or parent which supports the child to develop a sense of self and link the real world and the child's inner world.

Resilience

Empowering a child through choice-making promotes self-esteem and encompasses a therapeutic approach to supporting learning in the early years. Children are encouraged to express their emotions, negative or positive, within the social and environmental boundaries of the setting. Children are supported to identify and understand their feelings, to link choices and consequences, and to learn how to self-regulate their behaviour. As children learn how to moderate their levels of stress or emotional arousal, then **a window of tolerance** is created which allows children to capitalise on the learning opportunities which are available to them.

Many years ago, behaviour management highlighted negative behaviour to the child, with an implicit assumption that the child would be able to fulfil the adult's expectations by showing positive behaviour. Research on brain development and behaviour has given deeper insight into the education and care of young children within services or family home. Parenting programmes currently focus upon the promotion of positive behaviour through recognition of achievements and through the minimisation of negative behaviour by the use of choice-giving and consequences. For example, if 2-year-old Rory is climbing on the sofa, then the practitioner says, 'Rory, feet on the floor.' This instruction is constructive, and it is easy for a 2-year-old to understand and to follow. An alternative approach in which the practitioner says, 'No Rory, don't climb on the sofa,' gives a confusing message to a young child. The 2-year-old will appreciate that his behaviour is being criticised, but he may not have the capacity or ability to identify behaviour which would be acceptable. If practitioners use the word 'No' preceding the promotion of boundaries, it can create a barrier to the child learning and remembering social rules. It can also result in a child being dependent on an adult to regulate the child's behaviour.

Selective mutism

Selective mutism is a rare anxiety disorder which can be supported by the use of a therapeutic approach to learning. This disorder results from the effect of genetic, temperamental, environmental, and developmental factors. Children experience a chronic anxiety reaction in specific social situations which can be described as a phobia of speaking; however, these children are able to speak fluently and confidently in other circumstances. Recent research has indicated that the disorder affects one child out of every 100, and it is linked to immigration, bi-lingualism, and trauma (Hua & Major, 2016). Selective mutism can cause significant social and academic impairment due to the limitation that the phobia imposes on the child's learning opportunities and ability to interact. A therapeutic approach supports children to gain an understanding of themselves; an increase in self-confidence minimises their reaction to stress, which facilitates their ability to communicate verbally.

Children can benefit from therapeutic play by learning to identify an attachment figure, to decide when and how to access help, to make choices, and to understand their impact upon the world – physically, emotionally, and intellectually. Research indicates that resilience to adversity increases as they are effectively supported to deal with failure, to recognise achievement, and to create and implement their plans (Baldry & Moscardini, 2010).

Nurture classes, nurture rooms, nurture corners, and nurturing

The importance of emotional maturity and a child's ability and capacity to engage in learning activities has been actioned since the 1960s in the UK in the form of **nurture classes**. These classes were first introduced to primary schools in a deprived area of East London. Nurture classes in schools originally provided care and education for children who presented in primary 1 with emotional and social immaturity. Children attended the nurture classes for part of the school day and main classroom for the remainder of the 1–3 terms. The school work was presented within a structured planned environment, in small groups of mixed ages, and a trained nurture teacher plus support assistant would respond to the children's emotional needs alongside the formal schoolwork.

The nurture group is based upon the following principles (Boxall & Lucas, 2002):

- Learning opportunities should relate to the developmental stage of each child
- Behaviour is a child's demonstration of need and emotional status
- Nurturing supports the development of self-esteem
- Language is a tool which promotes communication and comprehension between child and adult
- The environmental space promotes safety to the child
- Transitions impact upon development and should be managed appropriately.

Over time the rationale of nurture classes has been used to develop practice in different contexts. The term **restorative experience** is often used. It has been recognised that some children have an immature sense of self, and the provision of nurturing gives children opportunities to develop self-confidence, self-esteem, and the ability to make social choices and to develop positive relationships. The intervention is beneficial for groups of children with social and emotional immaturity, and, currently, nurture classes in the UK can be accessed by children throughout primary school. There are innovative applications of nurturing for the oldest primary children, and these nurture classes/areas are often identified by the child's representation – for example, a **chill-out zone**.

Early years' settings introduced **nurture rooms** for pre-school children a few years ago. The nurture practitioner participates in the same nurture training as primary teachers, and the philosophy is to provide early intervention at a stage of learning which gives optimum preparation for the child's transition into formal schooling. Nurture rooms in nurseries have evolved, and some settings have established a **nurture corner** within a main playroom. Groups of children receive specific social and emotional support through planned activities with a nurture practitioner, but it has been recognised that all children benefit from interaction with workers in small group sessions which can be termed **nurturing**. The nurture corners represent a quiet area within a busy environment in which any child can relax and reaffirm a secure attachment relationship with a keyworker.

Education, care of children, and training of practitioners is formalised in the twenty-first century. This provides a structure for practitioners to use in planning, implementing, and evaluating activities and experiences for children's learning in accordance with national standards. Research has established the factors for supporting children's care, learning, and development. Moyles, Adams, and Musgrove (2002) detail training requirements for practitioners including extensive child development knowledge. The Department for Education and Skills (2007) promotes the incorporation of leaders with high qualifications. Sylva et al. (2007) identify sustained shared thinking between practitioners and children by using techniques such as modelling, questioning and demonstrating, and adhering to a relative balance of active and structured learning. Siraj-Blatchford et al. (2003) note that education and social development should be complementary.

Professionalism brings accountability, and this has led to checklists being used to identify and record a child's stage of development in relation to the average. A checklist can be informative but may result in each aspect of the child's development being recorded and assessed separately. This process can affect a professional's ability to view development holistically. The process also exposes the expertise or weaknesses of the practitioner's skills. A trail of information should be apparent from the initial observation of a child to assessment, planning and implementation of the curriculum, evaluation, and next steps. The trail reveals areas for continuous professional development for the practitioner.

Qualifications and registration impose professionalism to practitioners, but the implementation of new practices can engender disillusionment and affect self-assurance in experienced practitioners. The positive attributes of *new* best practice may be delivered as a direct comparison to the negative effects of previous practices – for example, child-led play as opposed to child-centred or child-structured and adult-led play. Childcare and education is a vocational profession. It is important that practitioners who have invested their personality and passion into the role are reassured that practices delivered to each generation of children are appropriate, within the context of society's expectations of childhood at that time. The unity and success of a team can be affected by challenges and insecurities felt by experienced and newly qualified practitioners in relation to old and new methods. An understanding of research and the route to change will support practitioners during the transition. It is useful to publicise and implement new practices as evolvement of previous methods of teaching and learning by acknowledging and valuing the contribution and experience of all practitioners.

National practice models guide practitioners to comprehend the child's world and potential influences from ecological systems. The traditional nursery nurse worked within the confines of his or her discipline; however, the early years' practitioner is part of a multi-disciplinary team of professionals.

The integrated team provides a rich forum for sharing information, explaining mitigating circumstances, assessing risks, deciding upon plans, agreeing and re-evaluating, reflecting, learning, and celebrating achievement with parents. One aspect is promoting resilience to potential adversities which could occur throughout a lifespan and could create a barrier to learning and development. Child-led pedagogy and a therapeutic approach respond to this need by helping the practitioner to use 'cultural sensitivity' in the implementation of curriculum, interventions, and the creation of a keyworker-child and practitioner-parent relationship. Cultural sensitivity is the response to each child's or parent's interpretation and resultant perception of his or her world. Perceptions affect actions and behaviour, and personalised responding by an early years' practitioner is **culturally aware practice**.

Child protection is *everyone's responsibility*. Comprehension of this concept has changed in the last 20 years, which has re-defined the early years' worker's role, identity, and responsibilities. Every child who attends an early years' service is currently supported by a team of professionals – for example, keyworker, playroom team, senior worker, and nursery manager, health visitor, health support team, and practice manager. If the context requires that a child is directly protected from harm by removing or minimising negative influences, then a team of named key professionals and parents is formed for every child. Members of this core group or integrated team fit the criteria of relevance and may include workers from health, education, social work, voluntary sector, police, housing, parents, and carers as appropriate. The early years' worker is a valued member of this integrated team.

References

Baldry, H., & Moscardini, L. (2010). *Letting the children lead – a final report to the Robertson Trust*. Glasgow: University of Strathclyde.

Bowlby, J. (1979). *The making and breaking of affectional bonds*. Abingdon: Routledge.

Boxall, M., & Lucas, S. (2002). *Nurture years*. London: Sage.

Bratton, S., Landreth, G. L., Kellam, T., & Blackard, S. R. (2006). *Child parent relationship therapy treatment manual: A 10 session filial therapy model for training parents*. New York: Routledge.

Central Advisory Council for Education. (1967). *Children and their primary schools ('the plowden report')*. London: HMSO.

Department for Children, Schools and Families. (2009). *Common assessment framework*. Retrieved March 11, 2009, from www.dcsf.gov.uk/everychildmatters/strategy/deliveringservices1/caf/cafframework

Department for Education and Skills. (2000). *The early years' foundation stage: Effective practice: Parents as partners*. London: HMSO.

Department for Education and Skills. (2007). *Aiming high for children: Supporting families*. London: HMSO.

Edmunds, L., & Stewart-Brown, S. (2003). *Assessing emotional and social competence in primary school and early years' settings: A review of approaches, issues and instruments*. Oxford: Institute of Health Sciences.

Erikson, E. (1999). *History – human development in a social context*. Retrieved July 2016, from www.erikson.edu/about/hisotry/erik-erikson/

Fonagy, P. (1999). Memory and therapeutic action. *The International Journal of Psycho-Analysis, volume 84, issue 3*. London: Routledge.

Fonagy, P., Gergely, G., & Target, M. (2007). The parent-infant dyad and the construction for the subjective self. *Journal of Child Psychology and Psychiatry, volume 48, number 3*, 314. Oxford: Blackwell Publishing.

Goldschmied, E., & Jackson, S. (1985). *People under three-young children in day care*. London: Routledge.

Hua, A., & Major, N. (2016). Selective mutism. *Current Opinion in Paediatrics, volume 28, number 1*. Retrieved July 2016, from http://ovidsp.uk.ovid.com/sp-3.20.0b/

Laevers, F. (1994). *The project experiential education: Concepts and experiences at level of context, process and outcome*. Studia Paedagogica: Leuven University.

Macleod-Brudenell, I., Cortvriend, V., Hallet, E., Kay, J., & Walkup, V. (2004). *Advanced early years' care and education levels 4 and 5*. Oxford: Heinemann.

Moyles, J. R. (1989). *Just playing? The role and status of play in childhood education*. Maidenhead: Open University Press.

Moyles, J. R., Adams, S., & Musgrove, A. (2002). *Study of pedagogical effectiveness in early learning: (speel)*. London: HMSO.

Oxford University Press. (1999). *The concise Oxford dictionary* (10th ed.). Oxford: Oxford University Press.

Scottish Executive. (1999). *A curriculum framework for children aged 3 to 5*. Dundee: Learning and Teaching Scotland.

Scottish Executive. (2004). *A curriculum for excellence*. Edinburgh: Scottish Executive.

Scottish Executive. (2005). *Birth to three: Supporting our youngest children*. Dundee: Learning and Teaching Scotland.

Scottish Government. (2008). *A guide to getting it right for every child*. Edinburgh: Scottish Government.

Scottish Government. (2010). *Pre-birth to three: Positive outcomes for Scotland's children and families*. Edinburgh: Scottish Government.

Siraj-Blatchford, I., Sylva, K., Taggart, B., Melhuish, E., Sammons, P., & Elliot, K. (2003). *The effective provision of pre-school education (EPPE) project (1997–2003)*. Nottingham: DfES.

Surestart. (2002). *Birth to three matters framework*. London: Paul Chapman Publishing.

Sylva, K., Taggart, B., Siraj-Blatchford, I., Totsika, V., Ereky-Stevens, K., Gilden, R., & Bell, D. (2007). Curricular quality and day-to-day learning activities in pre-school. *International Journal of Early Years Education, volume 15, number 1*, 49–65. London: Routledge.

Thomas, G., & Loxley, A. (2001). *Deconstructing special education and constructing inclusion*. Buckingham: Open University Press.

Trevarthan, C., & Aitken, K. J. (2001). Infant intersubjectivity: Research, theory, and clinical applications. *Journal of Child Psychology and Psychiatry, volume 42*. Cambridge: Cambridge University Press.

Welsh Assembly Government. (2004). *The foundation phase (3–7)*. Retrieved October 29, 2007, from http://accac.org.uk/eng/content.php?mID=655

2 Keyworker and child relationship

This chapter explains the importance of the keyworker to child relationships in the context of current research, theory, and the link to practice. Knowledge and understanding of secure and insecure attachment in children is necessary to professional development within early years. Research has linked relationships which are created in the child's earliest years with a blueprint which informs relationships throughout a lifespan. The ability and capacity to embrace learning opportunities is associated with positive relationships between a developing person who may be a child or adult and an attachment figure.

Theory can enhance practice by clarifying meaning and promoting understanding of behaviour, actions, and emotions of service-users and professionals. Acquisition of this deep-level of learning results in professionals practising with purpose, intent, and consistency over time. The chapter also explains the theory of mind which can be established within the first five years of childhood; however, lack of appropriate developmental opportunities can lead to an immature sense of the autobiographical self. This outcome affects the ability to understand and to accept the expectations of others, which is a prime consideration for social development and regulation of behaviour.

The earliest relationships

A starting point in understanding human relationships is to consider development from the moment of conception. Research from the field of neuroscience has greatly enhanced the knowledge of multi-disciplinary professionals. Evidence from 3-D models and brain scans has transformed our comprehension and given clarity to the processes of brain development which were previously hypothetical.

It is known that development before birth is affected by the influence of environmental factors upon the mother and her physiology (National

Scientific Council on the Developing Child, 2008, 2014). For example, physical or mental ill-health in an expectant mother will directly affect development of the unborn child. Physical ill-health has been linked to disease, inappropriate diet, the use of addictive substances, or passive exposure to toxins. Additionally, the effects of stress in a mother may be replicated in the unborn child due to stress hormones crossing the placenta. Raised levels of cortisol lead to high blood pressure and prolonged rapid heartbeat, which may affect mother and baby.

Babies have a genetic disposition to seek relationships from birth, and attachment behaviours are regarded as a baby's actions which are used to initiate, to retain, or to re-gain emotional and physical contact with a chosen individual (Bowlby, 1979); however, adverse circumstances may affect the creation of this relationship with a primary carer. The primary carer is usually the mother, the father, or the individual who has daily responsibility for the baby.

Ill-health in a new-born baby may necessitate adults prioritising a baby's physical care as opposed to emotional responding. Additionally, a baby who is unwell may not have the capacity or ability to actively seek an attachment relationship at birth. For example, foetal abstinence syndrome or indeed any abnormality may result in a baby focusing inwards in order to cope with physical needs. A baby who is ill may become self-absorbed and unable to react or interact with the proximal environment or carers. Nature demands that physical survival is given precedence before emotional wellbeing. This self-absorption creates a barrier or delay to the baby seeking an attachment figure, and a primary carer may not recognise the limited attachment cues as demonstrated by an infant who is in poor health; therefore, responses are limited.

Stress

Research has linked stress in childhood to physical and mental ill-health in adulthood (National Scientific Council on the Developing Child, 2016). Human beings secrete cortisol at a high rate in the earliest part of the day and lower towards evening. Cortisol is a hormone which supports the body to react quickly to stressful situations by regulating the immune system, inflammatory reactions, and the level of glucose in the blood. Unusual patterns of cortisol secretion may occur in children who experience trauma, and this ultimately has an adverse effect upon the body physically and emotionally. Hyperarousal or dissociation may be represented by behaviour relating to fight/flight or freeze response. Effective intervention should respond to the needs of each child and the child's unique responses to the learning environment. Furnivall and Grant (2014) identified three distinct stages of developmentally relevant, phased intervention to support children who have experienced trauma. These stages incorporate the creation of a safe environment and ensuring that the child *feels* safe, promoting self-regulation of emotions and resilience to adversities.

The brain has a capacity to create positive links between sensory experiences, objects, and a secure attachment relationship. Research has shown that neural connections can be supported to change throughout a lifespan, although the brain is most receptive in the birth to 3-year age group. Young children can be supported to understand themselves through sensory nurturing. Tactile and rhythmic experiences reminiscent of those felt by younger children can be offered to older children who are attempting to gain an understanding of self which has been blocked by trauma. Daily activities such as hair-brushing, massage, sand-play or water-play with bubbles, and nail-painting are useful representations of those early sensory experiences. Challenging behaviour may be exhibited by a child *because* the response from the adult is predictable. The situation is familiar and gives some control to the child as the adult fulfils expectations. It is essential that practitioners discuss children in their care through informal collegiate meetings and within formal support and supervision, in order to understand negativity, promote positivity, and maintain good mental health and professional resilience.

Stress can be represented and understood within three contexts. **Positive stress** is a mild, short-term reaction to common experiences in daily living. There is slight raising of cortisol levels, but regulation of this type of stress is achievable by the individual. **Tolerable stress** has the potential to disrupt brain architecture, but positive attachment relationships can provide the appropriate support for this stress to be time-limited and for the brain to recover. **Toxic stress** is prolonged activation of the body's stress responses. This type of stress can occur if a support mechanism is not available, and it leads to persistent elevation of stress hormones, which potentially impact upon physical and mental health.

Example from practice

At the beginning of my career, I started working with tiny babies who were withdrawing from the effects of addictive substances, as used by mothers during pregnancy. The medical care of such babies has progressed greatly over time, but the emotional impact of maternal addiction upon the new-born baby has not changed.

28 Keyworker and child relationship

> *I observe these infants distracted by physical discomfort, restless, reluctant to feed, and hard to settle, which minimises the capacity to make eye contact with primary carers. A young baby will cry for support as a reaction to internal discomfort, but inability to follow up this verbal signalling of need with eye contact to a primary carer reduces the effect of the attachment cue. Subsequently, reciprocity is not established between baby and carer. The dance of reciprocity refers to the complementary patterns of action and reaction which are apparent between carers and babies in a relationship of secure attachment.*
>
> *A lack of attachment cues leads to mothers losing confidence in exhibiting their parenting skills. Opportunities to nurture the attachment relationship decrease, and the inherent disposition for a baby to seek an attachment figure is not activated. Ambivalent or avoidant attachment may become the norm between these babies and their parents.*

However, the last ten years have seen a practical change to the focus of care for new-born babies within hospitals, particularly babies who have poor health. Effects from the local environment around the babies' cots have been studied and responded to, in order to minimise negativities and to promote protective factors. Parents, medical staff, and researchers have been given opportunities to work together in order to develop a hospital environment which suits the needs of babies. Lighting, equipment noise, and familiar and unfamiliar human voices are factors which have been identified as influential to the new-born baby's emotional, social, and, ultimately, physical wellbeing. Simple strategies of covering a cot to provide respite from fluorescent lighting contribute to creating an ambient atmosphere.

Parents and professionals often discuss a baby's wellbeing in the vicinity of the cot, which can result in the baby being exposed to emotive conversations by familiar family voices. Conducting these conversations away from the immediate area of a cot has been effective in maintaining tranquillity, which contributes to the physical and emotional health of a young baby.

Kangaroo-care is a term used to describe skin-to-skin contact between a parent and baby. Hospital staff actively encourage this demonstration of attachment by mother and father or extended family. This approach to the care of children in their earliest days has been a positive factor in activating the pre-disposition for attachment in a baby who has ill-health and emotional immaturity which subsequently prompts responsive behaviour from a primary carer.

It used to be believed that the hunger-system and the attachment-system were the same. Behavioural analysis led to an assumption that babies sought an attachment relationship in the quest for food, but anthropological research on monkeys which have a similar social system to humans has indicated that the systems are separate. A baby monkey will gravitate towards or favour a human being who offers comfort and nurturing to a human exclusively offering food (National Scientific Council on the Developing Child, 2008, 2014).

Bowlby (1979) described food from a theoretical perspective as being on the periphery of a child's attachment to a main carer. The separation of hunger and attachment systems grants significance to the development and maintenance of secure attachment in the evolution of human relationships. There is sometimes confusion between attachment theory and dependency theory.

Attachment theory

Attachment theory is characterised by the following factors as promoted by Bowlby (1979) and interpreted in terms of practice in the early years:

- Specificity
- Duration
- Ontogeny
- Engagement of emotion
- Learning
- Organisation
- Biological function
- Behaviour of primary carer.

Specificity: the child demonstrates attachment behaviour towards carers who have particular relational significance by seeking out contact through verbal and physical means.

Example from practice

It has been shown that babies will turn towards human faces within minutes of birth. A new-born baby will already be familiar with the sound of his or her mother's voice from the perspective of the womb, and soon after birth a baby will respond to this auditory stimulus by turning his or her head. Over time a baby will also respond to the sounds of other carers and supplement a head turn with crying, gurgling, and raising the arms in the expectation of affirmation of the relationship. This

30 *Keyworker and child relationship*

whole-body response to stimulus, as opposed to head-turning, contributes to a child's understanding of 'self.'

Duration: the attachment relationship lasts for a lengthy period and may continue throughout a lifespan.

Ontogeny: the first few years are regarded as important to provide a base for learning throughout a lifetime.

Example from practice

Research has indicated that the first 1,000 days of a baby's life (birth to 3 years of age) are regarded as a sensitive period for learning. The brain has been genetically programmed to seek out learning opportunities, to consolidate and apply knowledge in different circumstances, to problem-solve, and to identify a relevant source of support. The secure attachment relationship with a primary carer, and also relationships with secondary carers in settings, supports this brain development. The knowledge of these initial relationships in childhood creates models of attachment which influence relationships throughout a lifespan – for example, relationships with peers, partners, and professionals.

Engagement of emotion: an attachment relationship progresses through different stages – for example, creation, maintenance, potential disruption, and renewal. Behaviour which accompanies this relationship is influenced by intensive emotions.

Example from practice

Through discussion I have found that many parents are unaware of their natural skills in promoting emotional literacy to their children from birth. The first stage of achieving emotional literacy is recognition, differentiation, and verbal description of emotions. A new-born baby is placed in his or her mother's arms, and the birth mother, albeit tired and potentially overwhelmed by the circumstances, instinctively notices her baby's reaction to the world and tracks the baby's emotions alongside his or her behaviour. 'You seem so upset, you must be hungry. I can see that you are happy to meet your mum and dad. You look surprised. Are the lights too bright for you?' The dance of reciprocity commences.

Teaching of emotional literacy is a common feature in nurseries and schools. Children are given opportunities and guidance in understanding the link between emotions, expressing feelings through the use of descriptors, and the self-regulation of behaviour. The outcome of a child understanding his or her contribution to the world through purposeful and socially appropriate interactions contributes to achievement of the autobiographical self.

Learning: patterns of behaviour are influenced by expectation of the responses which are given by a primary carer. A baby or child will quickly associate cues and actions. Deep-level learning occurs when the attachment relationship is secure.

Example from practice

Parents describe the familial attachment relationship between children and their primary carers as 'unconditional love.' Practitioners identify the professional-child relationship as being created for a specific purpose, which is to support learning and development.

Organisation: attachment behaviour is instinctive in the early years, which results from an emotional need. Throughout childhood and adulthood, people continue to demonstrate the need for attachment in relation to stress or distress – for example, as a response to pain or confusion or fear. The patterns of behaviour which evolve within the dyad of child/ adult and carer reflect the family culture or organisational culture in the context of a setting.

Biological function: attachment theory describes these behaviours as functional for survival of the human species. It is a system which promotes physical safety and mental and emotional wellbeing.

Behaviour of primary carer: it takes two to make a relationship. Behaviour of child and carer perpetuates the secure or insecure attachment status.

Dependency theory

Dependency theory is characterised by the development of a **false sense of self**. This representation can lead to an unstable personality and emotional insecurity. Dependency occurs when a child does not seek his or her own interpretation of the world but refers to the knowledge and understanding of another person. This comprehension will influence the child's actions and behaviour.

Professionals will sometimes describe this situation as 'a child leading his life through his parent or sibling.' Adults may unconsciously

32 *Keyworker and child relationship*

contribute to this dependency by directing the child's actions and dismissing his or her reactions. A sense of self develops from emotional and intellectual interaction with the world. If a child adopts another person's interpretation and emotional reaction to situations, then a false sense of self develops.

Relationships and development

There has been an increase in awareness of influential factors upon a child's development over the last century which includes relationships between parents and professionals created in the child's early years. About 50 years ago, Montessori (1964) had acknowledged the significance of interaction between parents in their role of primary carers and professionals as secondary carers, by promoting formal information sharing sessions. Positive relationships between parents and professionals are currently associated with the success of interventional strategies.

The topic was researched in a long-term study on the effect of multiple carers on children's developmental progress (Siraj-Blatchford, Sylva, Muttock, Gilden & Bell, 2002). This study was called the Effective Provision of Pre-school Education Project (Department for Education and Skills, 2004). The research method included a review of case studies which highlighted the existence and purpose of a special relationship between a parent and professional. This relationship was defined by parent and professional having the same understanding of a child's educational needs and applying similar responsive strategies to support learning and development; therefore, an important outcome of the parent-professional relationship is consistency of care to a child.

The development of relational skills by professionals has been publicised to the workforce as an integral component of practice (Department for Children, Schools and Families, 2009; Scottish Government, 2008). A relationship is regarded as being established by interactions between a parent and professional for a specified purpose:

- Assessment of circumstances
- Information exchange
- Implementation of action plans
- To promote parental engagement with services.

Relationships in childhood and adulthood

Relationships which are formed throughout our lives can impact upon our ability and capacity to respond to learning opportunities. This chapter describes formation of relationships in the child's earliest years, and it uses practice examples to illustrate the effect of secure or insecure attachment upon achievement of potential. Links are made from these relational influences to adult relationships in a context of child protection. Terms which are specific to this area of learning are applied and explained to inform practice. Terminology which is used within a context of theory and research can be regarded as a barrier to understanding by practitioners, but this source of knowledge should be accessible to early years' workers in order to enhance their professional skillsets.

Secure attachment is necessary to encourage learning by promoting mental wellbeing which supports socio-personality development and positive interaction with environments. Bowlby (1979) referred to an attachment bond with a main person as providing a secure base for a child to engage in learning activities, and he applied the term of specificity to indicate a child's preference for a few individuals within the early years of life. Bowlby also noted that attachments could be reorganised in priority to personal preference or replaced at any point in childhood or adulthood. Human relationships have the potential for change throughout our lifespans.

A relationship between two human beings is a unique, emotive connection which supports emotional, social, and intellectual development. The need for an attachment figure has relevance throughout life; however, early representational models gain dominance. Attachment experiences which are acquired during the earliest years create a template which influences the formation of relationships in later life. Childhood relationships affect the creation of friendships in teenage years and impact upon early adulthood. Relationships influence wellbeing and, subsequently, performance and integration into social and learning environments – for example, further education, employment, and lifelong partnerships. The effect of the relationship blueprint can be passed from one generation to another, parent to child. Implementation of a role in the workplace can be affected too, from basic-grade workers to senior management, and this influence from practice can shape the pedagogy of an organisation.

Outcomes of insecure attachment were published in a report which highlighted the negative effect upon adult learning. The California Adverse Childhood Experience Study accessed 17,000 participants (Sroufe, Egeland, Carlson & Collins, 2005, 2006). Findings indicated that adults who had experienced adversity in childhood developed insecure attachment and subsequently demonstrated a propensity to mental health issues, crime, and underachievement in education.

Keyworker and child relationship

Purpose of a relationship

The primary carer is usually a parent or birth-family member, and the secondary carer is a professional in the context of services. A relationship between a child and a primary or secondary carer has two outcomes:

1. The relationship fulfils a condition for learning and development by supporting a child's understanding of himself or herself and facilitates positive interaction with the environment.
2. A relationship formed in the earliest years provides a benchmark of knowledge and experience which is applied to support and inform the formation of relationships throughout life.

These two outcomes of a relationship are based upon the premise of secure attachment which necessarily incorporates a human being's ability and capacity to identify a potential attachment figure and to respond to relational cues. The majority of children acquire the skill to control impulses, respond to social boundaries, and manage negative emotions at an elementary level, prior to attending school, through support of a responsive care-giver. Behaviour management techniques by parents may affect the child-primary carer attachment relationship, but this cycle, termed **rupture and repair**, is common. Children learn that relationships can be sustained or resumed, although the demonstration of attachment may change albeit for a brief period.

If experience of a secure attachment is not gained in a child's earliest years, then the child will find it difficult to manage trauma in childhood, as a young person, and throughout adulthood (Furnivall & Grant, 2014). The effects from adversities are most likely to be sustained if the sources are related to frequent repeated circumstances – for example, domestic violence or illicit drug use.

Early years' services are beginning to adopt the therapeutic approach to behaviour management in which an adult acknowledges the child's feelings as a basis for promoting understanding to the child in order to replace negative behaviours. This response by the adult can be termed **mind mindedness** and contributes to the child's development of the theory of mind.

I have observed many children, parents, and professionals throughout my career, and I have recorded common examples to illustrate links between theory and practice. Practitioners should use theory and practice to complement one another and to continuously seek knowledge and deeper insight into workplace actions.

Secure attachment in practice

Seven-year-old Lucy approaches the classroom door on a Monday morning. Her head is held high, and she glances mischievously at a friend in the school line. Lucy swings her arms in eager anticipation as the school day is about to unfold. This young schoolgirl makes the transition into her learning environment and halts for a few moments as she notices that the classroom layout has been changed. The familiar groups of four have become islands of eight tables and chairs. New fluorescent pens and large sheets of sugar paper take centrepiece on each activity station.

Lucy quickly identifies her name tag on a desk, and she confidently takes ownership of her newly allocated area: bag tucked under the desk, cardigan on the chair, pencil case positioned as Lucy chooses. This pupil is ready to learn.

Lucy has a secure attachment with her main carer, her mother. Attachment theory indicates that this emotional status within a relationship promotes a secure base for learning.

What does this mean in theory and practice?

Family relationships are role models for child-teacher school relationships.

Lucy's experience and expectations of a relationship have been gained from her family. She uses this knowledge, ways of building or negotiating her relationships, and understanding of self and others within the context of the school classroom – peers and teacher. Lucy knows that when she asks her mother a question, the response will be given with eye contact, interest, support, and time. This gives Lucy the expectation of a similar response from her teacher.

Family relationships are role models for friendships and peer relationships.

Lucy knows that when she is playing with her sister, she has to consider her sister's wishes, she has to negotiate, and she has to view the world from a sibling's perspective as well as her own. This gives Lucy the expectation of similar responses from her peers.

Development of the autobiographical self

- Lucy has knowledge of her world and develops an ability to be an active participant in her environment: physically, intellectually, communicatively, socially, and emotionally.
- Lucy learns how to cope with change by embracing new challenges.
- Lucy learns how to transfer knowledge, understanding, and skills from one environment to another, despite unpredictable circumstances.

36 *Keyworker and child relationship*

Expectations support and reinforce actions

The class teacher emphatically communicated her positive expectations of Lucy: 'Lucy can be relied upon in the classroom. Always smiling, always ready to respond and support the lesson plans.' This teacher had recognised the link between Lucy's positive presentation, her wellbeing, and her ability to cooperate and learn.

Readiness to learn

I observe Lucy swinging her arms as she approaches the classroom. This little girl demonstrates a physical awareness of her body as she expresses her positive emotions.

Lucy expects the learning environment to support her needs through reflecting upon memories of past experiences. This comprehension leads to rapid adaptation to the classroom changes, and potential barriers to learning for this child are minimised by Lucy's understanding of herself, which is based upon her secure attachment relationships. The outcome is Lucy's purposeful involvement with the learning environment in a context of emotional wellbeing.

The link from theory to practice indicates that secure attachment nurtures Lucy's readiness to learn.

- Lucy identifies her preferred learning style.
- Lucy learns how to seek out new knowledge.
- Lucy learns how to question and confirm understanding.
- Lucy learns how to say, 'I don't know / I can't understand/ please help me.'
- Lucy learns how to identify and celebrate her achievement.

Ambivalent attachment in practice

Three-year-old John approaches the playroom door; his mother has a hand on his shoulder. John runs across the threshold and into the den area. John's mother remains in the doorway and calls John to give her a hug. The little boy ignores his mother, but he is led back to her by the nursery keyworker. John receives a momentary hug from his mother; he clings to her legs but keeps his eyes averted. As soon as he is released, John returns quickly to the den area. John is not ready to learn; he has not made a positive transition from one learning environment (home) to another (nursery).

At pick-up time John's mother opens the playroom door, and the keyworker prompts John to go home. John's mother does not have any physical or verbal interaction with her son as she talks to the keyworker. John approaches the two adults and hits his mother. John's mother reprimands him and walks away into the cloakroom area. John follows.

John has ambivalent attachment to his main carer. The inherent desire for attachment is so strong that he continues to seek a response although his need is not met. The non-fulfilment of need results in John demonstrating a range of positive and negative behaviour in the quest for a secure relationship. John does not experience emotional wellbeing; therefore, he continues to use different behavioural strategies in an attempt to gain support for his needs.

John's knowledge and understanding of relationships at home provides a pattern and expectations of behaviour within the relationships with adults in the nursery environment. This young child does not know what to expect from a relationship, but he is instinctively using different behaviours in an attempt to gain order and predictability in his world.

What does this mean in theory and practice?

Expectations provide or remove learning opportunities for children.

- John has used two different strategies, positive and negative behaviours, to prompt an attachment response from his mother.
- His mother has not responded to these cues.
- John remains insecurely attached, and his attachment-seeking strategies are repeated on a daily basis and ultimately form patterns of behaviour.
- John has compartmentalised the environments within his life: home and nursery. He is not able to experience a positive transition by linking one area to another, as he demonstrated by running into the den corner in the nursery, eyes averted from his mother.
- The keyworker returned John to his mother in order to demonstrate 'social departing' between a child and parent. These responses are mistimed and do not meet the needs of John but simply follow rules of behaviour within this organisation.

Practitioners are reacting to behaviour rather than understanding the child's needs. Behaviour is an outcome of social and emotional development and of attachment status. Practitioners in this setting were inadvertently promoting these patterns by their expectations of John's behaviour. Comments from nursery are, 'John always behaves that way. I could have told you that he would do that. That's just John's way. He does not know any different. If you leave him alone then he'll settle down himself.'

38 Keyworker and child relationship

These practitioners were demonstrating knowledge of John's attachment status but a lack of understanding. Opportunities were being missed, on a regular basis, to support a vital area of learning for this child. A secure attachment relationship with a keyworker could have been nurtured in the nursery and impact upon the negative experiences from John's past. This child could have been supported to change his inner working model. The little boy's perceptions and expectations of his world could have been transformed.

These examples may appear to be inconsequential everyday occurrences; however, the interactions are highly significant and provide opportunities to nurture a secure attachment relationship between professional and child. This relationship will directly impact upon a learner's capacity and ability to achieve potential. There are multiple opportunities to affect attachment within practice, and the outcome can have a substantial impact upon the individual, peers, family, professionals, and subsequent generations.

Understanding of self

Insecure attachment affects the creation and maintenance of relationships in childhood and adulthood through the use of an inappropriate representational model. The demonstration of ambivalent attachment may incorporate an extreme display of misplaced positive or negative emotions – for example, a child may exhibit familiarity to strangers or aggression towards familiar adults.

Children are often attracted to new relationships – for example, with students on short-term placements. I have frequently observed children who have ambivalent attachment status demonstrating a desire to spend time with a student, wanting physical and emotional contact, and showing stress when the student leaves. Inexperienced students or practitioners may 'mirror' a child's emotions, thus reinforcing the emotional impact of this insecure attachment.

I have observed children with autism moving backwards to sit on the knee of a student. The student may be the adult in a room who is sitting still on a chair, in the early days of placement, unsure of the role. The qualified practitioner is busy 'working the room.' The child may appear to be seeking out physical comfort and attachment; however, the child may simply be using this opportunity to rest. The child may not be seeking attachment and may view the stationary student as part of the physical environment. I have observed the reaction from students who do not have the knowledge and understanding of attachment theory and the link to practice. Students can respond inappropriately to attachment cues through lack of direction from a workplace mentor; therefore, insecure attachment continues.

These incidents may go unnoticed in a busy playroom or classroom. It is the responsibility of practitioners to support all learners: children, parents, students, colleagues. Experienced practitioners should monitor and advise students or peers in this area of work. Often, students are given intensive support to plan, implement, and evaluate activities. Students frequently have their learning extended by mentors creating links from spontaneous interactions to the curriculum outcomes. Active learning is understood, but attachment cues and subsequently appropriate responses can be missed.

Secure attachment is the basis of learning, development, and achievement of potential. Howe (2008) linked ambivalent attachment to a negative understanding of self and inconsistent representation of others. Insecure attachment status was described by Thompson (2006) as a barrier which prevented, restricted, or negatively affected a human being's ability to embrace social experiences as represented in the example of John.

Avoidant attachment in practice

Five-year-old Wendy slowly approaches the line outside her classroom door. She willingly allows her peers to push in front of her. Wendy enters the classroom and dips her head so that her long straggly hair swings in front of her eyes as she passes the teacher. Wendy sits at her group and puts her hands in her pockets, eyes downcast: a typical presentation of a child with low self-esteem. A peer reminds Wendy to put her bag on the back of her chair. Wendy's bag falls to the floor, and she does not attempt to retrieve it, although she bites her lip and appears stressed by this event.

Wendy takes up her daily pose at the desk with legs tucked tightly under the chair, one hand twirling her long blond hair, the other hand near her mouth. Wendy frequently sucks her sleeve. This young pupil is not ready to learn.

This little girl has created a barrier to learning. She is avoiding relationships. Wendy demonstrates an immature understanding of her physical self. She has developed techniques in order 'not to be noticed.'

If needs are not met, then the desire to seek attachment diminishes over a period of time. Wendy is consciously suppressing attachment desires and developing practical strategies which create a barrier to demonstration of her emotions. This status is known as avoidant attachment.

What does this mean in theory and practice?

Role-modelling

- Wendy is regarded as an amenable placid child at home and school. Wendy's care arrangements are inconsistent and unpredictable. The main carers of this 5-year-old girl are her father, paternal grandmother or aunt, and, occasionally, temporary foster-carers. Throughout her early

childhood, Wendy sought out secure attachment relationships, but the adults who were available at that time were unable to recognise her cues or to give the necessary responses to support her emotional needs.
- Wendy has not been able to develop a model of 'how to create a secure relationship.'
- Wendy's understanding of her sense of self has become dependent on representation by others: a false sense of self.
- Instinct has provided Wendy with strategies which minimise the potential for a relationship to be developed and which contribute to behaviour patterns.
- This child is demonstrating avoidant attachment.

A false sense of self

Avoiding relationships gives Wendy a sense of control and predictability over her environment. It eliminates unmanageable and potentially distressing interactions with peers and adults. However, Wendy's interpretation and reactions within a learning environment restrict the opportunity for this young girl to experience a happy and fulfilling childhood and to prepare for relationships in adolescence and throughout her lifespan.

Howe (2008) indicated a link from avoidant attachment to an emotionally self-contained model of self in which others were regarded as hostile. Terms from practice describe the outward presentation of a child with avoidant attachment status – for example, still face or emotionless. These descriptors indicate a distinct lack of social engagement with the proximal environment. This represents Wendy's world.

Howe (2011) extended comprehension of the false sense of self by indicating that the use of an internal working model, which was based upon avoidant attachment, led to a human being adopting the emotions of others over a period of time; thus, the child or adult does not gain the skills to self-regulate his or her emotions. The resultant behaviour responds to the needs of others rather than personal needs. Wendy's behaviour and interaction with the learning environment depends on the teacher monitoring and directing her actions. Wendy has developed an expectation of this pattern of events occurring, and she can be observed looking at the teacher and hesitating as she awaits instruction. Wendy comforts herself through immature behaviours, sucking on her sleeve and demonstrating insecurity and uncertainty about what happens next. Wendy has limited practice in making choices.

- Wendy is not planning her interaction with learning opportunities.
- Wendy is not accessing prior knowledge and understanding to aid interpretation of situations.

- Wendy is not using her imagination and creativity.
- Wendy is not self-regulating her behaviour or emotions.
- Wendy is dependent on the adult.

A teacher describes Wendy as 'quiet and an easy pupil to have in class as she always does as she is told!' This teacher has focussed upon managing the classroom environment rather than Wendy's learning needs. Supporting children to self-regulate their behaviour contributes greatly to the management of a learning environment such as a classroom or playroom. Children become active, responsible participants, which reduces the necessity for management of behaviour.

Chaotic attachment in practice

Luke's family have been involved with child protection processes over two generations. Luke, who is 3 years old, is dropped off at nursery by a council care driver – this arrangement ensures regular attendance at nursery. Luke does not know this driver, and he quickly runs into the nursery as the driver signs the drop-off record.

Luke notices a new student, and he immediately seeks a physical response by leaning against her. The student talks to Luke, and he demonstrates nurturing behaviour with this unfamiliar adult. He touches the student's necklace, asking many questions, anxiously searching her face and seeking eye contact. One fist is clenched. Luke is tense and vigilant. The student turns to another child who has approached the scene. The student takes this child's hand, and together they build a tower of Lego bricks. Luke leans over and pulls the student's necklace in anger; he spits on the table and runs into the book corner.

What does this mean in theory and practice?

- Luke is unable to regulate his behaviour.
- He is using several strategies in his attempt to form a relationship with the student: nurturing a relationship/demonstrating aggression/withdrawing and avoiding.

This child is not ready to learn. He is demonstrating chaotic attachment. Fischer and Bidell (2006) described the fourth type of attachment as chaotic and linked the occurrence to victims of abuse and trauma. Inappropriate and appropriate representational models co-exist. Secure and insecure models of attachment may exist together and be used within the creation of one or more relationships. Howe (2008) described the self as bad and others regarded as frightening within this context. Human beings who experience chaotic attachment status form a barrier to the creation of a relationship, which is based upon negative perceptions of the world. This status is demonstrated by Luke through his behaviour and emotional reactions.

A simple but relevant learning experience is gained from the example of Luke. The keyworker was observed initiating the council care-driver to complete the drop-off record before she acknowledged Luke's presence within her learning environment, before she supported this vulnerable child to make an effective transition from home to nursery, and before she promoted re-affirmation of a secure attachment relationship. Managing oneself and prioritising tasks is the responsibility of every professional. Bureaucracy is essential within the context of child protection; however, in this common but important example, bureaucracy created a barrier between adult carer and developing child. Two minutes spent 'meeting and greeting' Luke in a timely manner which responded to his needs, before signing the attendance records, would have been invaluable to this child's emotional and social development, his expectations of familiar adults, and his ability to transfer from home to nursery. Legislation and guidance supports practitioners to identify, record, and understand adversities and protective factors upon each child which ultimately affect development. Some of these issues cannot be changed quickly, but **each day a child can be supported to gain resilience to life's challenges** and to develop skills and talents to minimise the negative effect of ecological influences.

When human beings enter different environments, there is a window of opportunity in which impressions are formed, self-esteem is raised or lowered, and a readiness to learn is activated or not. As children or adults, we all have insecurities and personal requirements to support our learning, particularly during transition periods. The following examples were observed recently at an international conference on attachment.

Example from practice

Professional learners

Before presenting to a group of professional learners in a conference, I observe the reactions and interactions as individuals make the transition from the informal coffee break in the foyer of a conference venue into the formality of the lecture theatre.

- *I observe adults anxiously seeking a familiar face in the crowd.*
- *I observe adults demonstrating tense body language and choosing a side stairway in order 'not to be noticed.'*

- *I observe adults sitting down, minimising physical movements, trying not to invade the space of an unknown neighbour, eyes averted.*
- *I observe adults gaining reassurance and confidence by interacting with a mobile phone – a familiar and predictable medium with which to access a contact list.*
- *I observe adults striding across in front of the podium, confident, interacting with myself in the role of presenter – making a quick impact upon their learning environment.*
- *I observe adults 'meeting and greeting' colleagues from past and present. Tenuous professional links become strong friendships in unfamiliar territory. The learning environment is perceived as attractive and welcoming in the company of a peer.*

Developing the autobiographical sense of self

Miell (1995) described an average 5-year-old child having an understanding of 'self' which can be termed 'the autobiographical self.' This concept encompasses the child's knowledge of physical attributes, gender, identity within the family unit, and comprehension of the existential self which enables a person to become an active participant in his or her environment. A consistent and predictable relationship with a care-giver is required to support this area of development for a child.

Fonagy, Gergely, Jurist, and Target (2002) identified five aspects of self as levels of understanding which are achieved within the first five years of life by the majority of children. Each level does not exist in isolation but represents points of reference for a child, which supports comprehension of the autobiographical self at 4 or 5 years of age. The first two levels demonstrate a basic development of self as a physical and a social agent which is determined by the child's interactions with a proximal and distal environment.

Example from practice

Nine-month-old Jen sits independently. She pats a ball by her side. Jen is using an instinctive reaction which has been triggered by the use of her senses of sight and touch. Her current emotional status is wellbeing, which supports her curiosity about this proximal environment. The ball rolls forward. Jen stretches towards this moving object, flips onto her tummy, and adjusts her position quickly, legs uncurled, head up, arms forward, ready to learn. The little girl lies prone as she uses both hands to reach the target.

A keyworker sits on the floor a few metres from Jen. She tracks Jen's actions verbally, smiling and encouraging the infant's mobility.

Jen seeks out eye-contact with this secondary carer, then the little girl quickly re-focuses upon her chosen goal, the ball. Jen's eye movements signal her needs and desires to the adult. The keyworker responds to the cues and nudges the ball towards Jen, just out of reach to encourage the little girl's movements. Reciprocity is apparent, as is teamwork then concordant inter-subjectivity between adult and learner.

These strategies may appear to be inconsequential, everyday practice, but a deep level of understanding of these actions can be gained by linking practice to theory, and theory to practice. Reflection requires a practitioner to consider theory in order to enhance practice by an increase in knowledge and understanding. Reflection requires practitioners to consider their own practices so that theory can be used to give clarity to their roles and responsibilities.

- If a worker only reflects upon practice, then professional development is limited to reviewing personal past experiences.
- If a worker also uses theory to inform practice, then professional development can be realised in a range of circumstances and activate transferrable skills.

An increase in comprehension of practice gives significance to the person-to-person interactions between child and adult. For example, Jen's learning in this situation is profound and affects her future development. This child knows what she can achieve and, importantly, when she needs help to succeed. It is the beginning of a relational blueprint which assists little Jen to achieve potential by supporting her ability and capacity to identify attachment figures and to create secure relationships throughout her lifespan. The impact from these earliest experiences continues.

The third and fourth level of self requires a sophisticated environment, expectations, and responses from a primary care-giver:

- A teleological agent = a child who is able to understand cause and effect.
- An intentional mental agent = a child who is able to plan and to implement ideas.

Fonagy et al. (2002) referred to this period as a social-cognitive revolution. This means that the child gains an understanding of actions, purpose, and reactions and takes ownership of his or her role in interactions with the environment. Additionally, the child has knowledge of a power-base within social relationships and his or her control of the material (resources) environment. Development of self-esteem is linked to the child's realisation of this base and the child's acquisition of the third and fourth level of self.

Example from practice

Three-year-old Callum bends down to look at a shape-sorter. He turns his head to one side in order to see the multi-coloured shapes which are lying inside the red box. This little boy picks up the box and shakes it to confirm the presence of objects. Realising that shaking will not release the shapes, Callum taps the box on the floor as he considers the situation. This child is problem-solving by using his sight/hearing/touch. The 3-year-old learner identifies and seeks out a source of support, and he turns to his keyworker. The keyworker crouches down at Callum's eye-level; she extends her hands, palm upwards, and raises her eyebrows as she says, 'What would you like me to do?' This helps the learner to participate in forward planning through the verbal interaction. Callum's ideas are given importance by this simple request. The response by the keyworker passes power to Callum, maintaining the little boy's control of this situation. Callum requests, 'Open it!'

- Callum has predicted the box can be opened to release the shapes.
- Callum is forward planning.
- Callum has identified and accessed a reliable source of support, an attachment figure.
- Callum is changing his environment through interaction.
- Callum is demonstrating active learning.
- Callum has acquired knowledge of sequencing, cause, and effect which forms the basis for accessing many learning opportunities.

The final level of self is the following:

- A representational agent = links to the emergence of the autobiographical self.

Achievement of this final level is depicted in the previous example of Lucy who has secure attachment.

Theory of mind

Children have an inherent predisposition to seek out interaction with others. Babies are born with elementary skills of socialising, and the resulting intersubjectivity with another person creates a pathway for the development of theory of mind, cognition, language, and an understanding of the autobiographical self. Theory of mind was defined by Cicchetti and Toth (2006) as the shift from a situation-based to a representation-based understanding of behaviour. Practitioners recognise this important step as a child's ability to participate in imaginative play. Development of the theory of mind includes a child's capacity to comprehend that individuals may have different thoughts about the same situation. This knowledge and understanding is essential to social interactions throughout childhood, adolescence, and adulthood and to self-regulation of behaviour.

Sympathy and empathy evolve from the theory of mind.

Sympathy originates from your personal perspective. It is giving support by using a base of knowledge and understanding which is gained from your own interpretation of your world. The use of sympathy entails comprehension of another person's experience by reflecting upon a similar personal experience. Emotions, actions, and behaviour are used to promote understanding by assuming that the other person has had the same or similar reactions.

Empathy relates to the perspective of another person. It is giving support by using a base of knowledge and understanding derived from the other person's perspective. Mirror neurons are activated in the brain when facial expressions and the body language of others are observed. This supports an emotional understanding which reflects the emotions of the other person. The use of empathy involves reflecting upon another person's experiences, behaviour, and emotions, as described or demonstrated by that individual, and responding verbally or physically in a manner which promotes understanding and care – the therapeutic relationship.

References

Bowlby, J. (1979). *The making and breaking of affectional bonds.* Abingdon: Routledge.
Cicchetti, D., & Toth, S. L. (2006). Developmental psychopathology and preventive intervention. In W. Damon & R. Lerner (Eds.), *Handbook of child psychology, volume 4* (pp. 511–512). Hoboken, NJ: John Wiley & Sons.
Department for Children, Schools and Families. (2009). *Common assessment framework.* Retrieved March 11, 2009, from www.dcsf.gov.uk/everychildmatters/strategy/deliveringservices1/caf/cafframework
Department for Education and Skills. (2004). *The effective provision of pre-school education (EPPE) project: The final report.* Nottingham: The Institute of Education.
Fischer, K. W., & Bidell, T. R. (2006). The bioecological model of human development. In W. Damon & R. M. Lerner (Eds.), *Handbook of child psychology, volume 1* (p. 377). Hoboken, NJ: John Wiley & Sons.
Fonagy, P., Gergely, G., Jurist, E., & Target, M. (2002). The development of an understanding of self and agency. In P. Fonagy (Ed.), *Affect regulation, mentalization and the development of self.* (pp. 203–251). New York: Other Press.

Furnivall, J., & Grant, E. (2014). *Insights: Trauma sensitive practice with children in care*. Glasgow: Institute for Research and Innovation in Social Services.

Howe, D. (2008). Relationship-based thinking and practice in social work. *Journal of Social Work Practice: Psychotherapeutic Approaches in Health, Welfare and the Community, volume 22, 45–56*. London: Routledge.

Howe, D. (2011). *Attachment across the life course, a brief introduction*. Basingstoke: Palgrave Macmillan.

Miell, D. (1995). The development of self. In P. Barnes (Ed.), *Personal, social and emotional development of children*. Blackwell: Open University.

Montessori, M. (1964). *The Montessori method*. New York: Schocken Books Inc. (Original work published 1912).

National Scientific Council on the Developing Child. (2008). *The timing and quality of early experiences combine to shape brain architecture, working paper 5*. Cambridge: Harvard University.

National Scientific Council on the Developing Child. (2014). *Excessive stress disrupts the architecture of the developing brain, working paper 3 updated*. Cambridge: Harvard University Press.

National Scientific Council on the Developing Child. (2016). *The science of early childhood development: Closing the gap between what we know and what we do*. Cambridge: Harvard University.

Scottish Government. (2008). *Early years and early intervention, a joint Scottish government and COSLA policy statement*. Edinburgh: Scottish Government.

Siraj-Blatchford, I., Sylva, K., Muttock, S., Gilden, R., & Bell, D. (2002). *Researching effective pedagogy in the early years, report number 356*. London: Department for Education and Skills.

Siraj-Blatchford, I., Sylva, K., Taggart, B., Melhuish, E., Sammons, P., & Elliot, K. (2003). *The effective provision of pre-school education (EPPE) project (1997–2003)*. Nottingham: DfES.

Sroufe, L. A., Egeland, B., Carlson, E., & Collins, W. A. (2005). *The development of the person: The Minnesota study of risk and adaptation from birth to adulthood*. New York: The Guilford Press.

Sroufe, L. A., Egeland, B., Carlson, E., & Collins, W. A. (2006). Placing early attachment experiences in developmental context. In K. E. Grossman, K. Grossman & E. Watters (Eds.), *Attachment from infancy to adulthood: The major longitudinal studies* (pp. 48–70). New York: The Guilford Press.

Thompson, R. A. (2006). The development of the person: Social understanding, relationships, conscience, self. In W. Damon & R. M. Lerner (Eds.), *Handbook of child psychology, volume 3* (pp. 24–35, 68–69, 78). Hoboken, NJ: John Wiley & Sons.

3 Child protection in the early years

This chapter discusses the complexity of early years' work, particularly with vulnerable families in a context of early intervention within mainstream services, and it clearly defines the concepts of felt, expressed, and normative needs in theoretical and practical terms. The chapter describes the development of the therapeutic relationship as a medium to support change and development of parenting skills so that a child may experience a positive childhood within a birth family culture. The context of child protection imposes parameters upon relationships between parents as service-users and an integrated team as the service-provider. The early years' practitioner is an integral member of this team. Teams are composed of professionals from the disciplines of health, education, social work, the voluntary sector, housing, and police. Parents may create relationships with professionals on a voluntary or mandatory basis. Both contexts are determined by legislation and guidance. Crises require timely solutions and exert pressures on professionals individually and collectively. Professionals working within a multi-disciplinary team can create respectful relationships and gain knowledge of roles without the unnatural influence of a crisis. The realisation of complementariness of skills within the team results in sound practice.

Theory

Knowledge of the theory of relationships is usually gained during undergraduate courses and potentially re-visited in post-graduate study. Theory is easy for professionals to access. Compulsory registration within each discipline has resulted in practitioners gaining entry to databases in order to source current and past research, significant case reviews, and countless bibliographies. Continuous professional development and registration to practice are dependent on the ability of each worker to accumulate a base of evidence which demonstrates practice relevant to a professional role; however, understanding which supports the optimum application of knowledge can only truly be achieved with experience of practice.

Theoretical framework

The Ecological Systems of Human Development (Bronfenbrenner, 1979, 2005) is often cited as an effective theoretical framework to support exploration and promote understanding of the influences which affect the development of human beings. Practice models throughout the United Kingdom refer to this framework within guidance (Department for Children, Schools and Families, 2009; Scottish Government, 2008). Guidance supports a professional to respond sensitively to individual needs of parents and children. A term which is applied to this approach is **personalised responding**.

The author of this theoretical framework, Urie Bronfenbrenner, was born in Russia in 1917 and brought up by his parents in America. Bronfenbrenner lived in a cottage in the grounds of a children's home which was set in many acres of farmland in the outskirts of New York. His father was a neuro-pathologist who was employed by the home to support the children and to conduct research in this environment. The residents were the childhood companions of Bronfenbrenner throughout his formative years. Each child was tested at entry to this residential establishment using the Stanford-Binet test and re-tested at set periods to contribute to the research data. Entry and exit from the home was dependent on the level of achievement. Bronfenbrenner had noticed that some children learned and developed within the environment and subsequently left the home; however, the majority of children demonstrated a decline in the results of the intelligence testing and remained as Bronfenbrenner's companions throughout childhood. This puzzled the boy, and he concluded, through discussion with his father, that human development is dependent on the individual's interpretation and reaction to internal and external influences. He also gained an awareness of the impact from society upon the individual as the results of the IQ test determined his friends' pathways as young children. This comprehension by the young Bronfenbrenner informed the creation of the Ecological Systems of Human Development and led to the simple format of four concentric circles to represent influences upon development.

Four systems were identified which encompassed potential influences. The inner circle as the **micro-system** is an environment in which children experience their first relationships and understanding of their world – the home. As children grow, their world is extended to include **multiple micro-systems** – learning situations outside the family unit. Children in the twenty-first century access many micro-systems – for example, nursery, school, leisure, care, and recreation facilities. Links may be created between these micro-systems which are termed **meso-systems**. An example is a teacher sharing knowledge with a parent regarding homework tasks which results in the parent implementing this understanding to the child in a home environment. The meso-system has created a bi-directional link between school, home, and back to school. The link incorporates information and attitude. The teacher is promoting positivity of education to the parent. This attitude has the potential to be reinforced to the child and extended family within the home environment. Dissemination of knowledge, understanding, and skills across micro-systems strengthens the power of the system to promote the child's development.

Life continues, and children are exposed to influences from the **exo-system**. These influences indirectly impact upon a child. An example can be given from circumstances which affect families today. If a parent is delayed at work and subsequently is late in collecting a child from 'after-school care,' then the influence from the parent's work has indirectly affected the child. A late pickup may result in take-away food as opposed to a home-cooked meal, a later bedtime, anxiety in the child, and, potentially, care from a parent who is tired and irritated by the change of routine. The final set of influences occur in the **macro-system**. The macro-system refers to formal factors which affect development – for example, local, national, and international policies and legislation.

In later years Bronfenbrenner (2005) presented this framework as the Bio-Ecological Systems of Human Development. This version refers to the impact of biology upon a human being. Bronfenbrenner recognised that biology affects growth and influences the potential of human beings; however, it is interaction with environments which allows that potential to be realised through learning and ultimately development. Bronfenbrenner and his father gained insight and understanding of human development by observing and interacting with children in the confines of a residential community of children and adults. This knowledge has provided the rationale for practice in current health, social work, education, and third-sector services (voluntary sector). If the influences are complementary, then a child will develop within a supportive network; however, if the influences impact upon the child in a chaotic and potentially random manner, then the system is disorganised and presents barriers to development.

Attachment

John Bowlby (1979) contributed to our understanding of human development by researching relationships. Bowlby identified the significant impact from a **secure or insecure attachment** upon an individual's capacity and ability to learn. Bowlby had focussed his research on relationships between a child and primary carer; however, the theory of attachment can be used to understand relationships between service-users and service-providers, as parents and professionals.

Relationships which are formed within the context of services are created by recourse to professional skill and personality of each worker. It takes confidence and expertise to maintain a parent-professional relationship in a context which encompasses barriers to positive interaction – for example, child protection may be perceived by the service-provider or service-user as promoting negativity upon the relationship (Whitters, 2015).

Child protection

The context of this chapter is child protection, and the response of services to children in need has changed over time. Historically, in the mid-1900s, child protection in the UK took a reactive approach. Society accepted that parents had the right to bring up their children within a birth-family culture, and there was an assumption that the majority of parents had the capacity and ability to fulfil this role. Services would intervene if evidence indicated that a child had been harmed emotionally or physically. The parent-professional relationship was subsequently created in a context subject to legislation and formal parameters.

The child was at the heart of policies and procedures in the 1980s and 1990s. The re-focusing debate on child protection led to a deeper understanding of this concept and subsequent changes in practice which are currently maintained in service-delivery (Department of Health, 1995; Parton, 2007; Scottish Executive, 1997). A development in the referral process included the potential for a parent's voluntary involvement with services, and it emphasised a shift from mandatory post-crisis intervention to a system of preventative work and a focus upon child welfare and achievement of potential. Pre-crisis intervention regards the resilience of a child as a protective factor in minimising the affects from adversities. The change was influenced by guidance and legislation which promoted the rights of the child in addition to the creation of parent-professional partnerships (United Nations Convention on the Rights of the Child (UNCRC), 1989). The parent-professional relationship is integral to this approach as a medium which supports change and development in order to increase each child's life-chances and to celebrate parenthood.

Policy and practice recognise that parents are a child's primary educators who can be supported to learn and develop within the parenting role – therefore representing protective factors rather than adversities to their child's development. The rights of each child direct decision-making and actions. The importance of the parenting role to children and of society's high valuation of the associative responsibilities are recognised in the National Parenting Strategy for Scotland 2012 (Scottish Government, 2012).

Society's perspective

Early intervention has been identified as a major contribution to child protection by supporting families to make a developmental transition from a negative destructive culture into mainstream society. A positive outcome can impact upon the individual, national and local community, and wider society. Governmental and local policy promote early intervention as a means to an individual achieving his or her potential and contributing to society as a responsible, effective citizen.

Practitioner's perspective

Relationship-based practice has been recognised in recent years as encompassed within the role of service-provider. Sudbery (2010) placed the responsibility for responding to each client's relational needs upon each practitioner. Documentation within practice models supports practitioners to represent adversities and protective factors in a format which enhances comprehension by linking theory and practice. Recording of vulnerability and resilience presents each child's interpretation and reaction to his or her world and provides a basis for creation of a child's personal care plan.

Edelman (2004) associated this responsibility with the organisation and put emphasis upon supervision programmes for practitioners to support the development of effective practice. Supervision was also raised by Howe (2008) as a necessary aspect of practice so that knowledge and understanding may be gained from behaviour, personality, and relationship styles in the parent-professional dyads.

Relationship-based practice

The Plowden Report from 1967 (Central Advisory Council for Education, 1967) promoted partnerships between parents and professionals in education, and subsequently this concept was introduced to training for Scottish and English social service and care sectors in 1997 (Care Sector Consortium, 1997). Working in partnership with parents became an evidential registration requirement for practitioners from health, education, and social work, and this approach is currently embedded within practice. Recent legislation in Scotland has renewed the focus upon the parent-professional relationship (Scottish Government, 2014a, 2014b).

Relationships are important influences upon the socio-emotional development and behaviour of humans (Howe, 2008). The parent-professional relationship is significant within a context of child protection as a medium which contributes to re-formation of a parent's understanding of self. Child protection involves supporting parents to view their child's world from a different perspective – therefore affecting the parents' actions, emotions, and behaviour.

The relational skill of a professional, which includes the creation of relationships in a child's earliest years, was recently identified as a criteria for a successful outcome from early intervention (Moullin, Waldfogel & Washbrook, 2014). Research on neglect of children indicated that the positive effects from early interventions could be sustained by good relationships between parents and professionals (Daniel, Burgess & Scott, 2012). This knowledge has been applied successfully in Scotland in the form of the Family-Nurse Partnership (Scottish Government, 2015). It is a model of preventative work which has been promoted since 2010, and initial results indicate a positive impact upon the protection of vulnerable children by intervening at an opportune period of childhood and parenthood. Practice responds to the needs of first-time teenage parents by using a voluntary relationship between young mother and health professional to implement early intervention. Strategies are based upon the physical and emotional health needs of child and parent.

The Family-Nurse Partnership aims to develop the intervention through integration with local services which respond to cultural needs of a community. Programmes which are implemented with cultural sensitivity have been identified as effective approaches to engaging parents and maintaining involvement over time (Moran, Ghate & van der Merwe, 2004).

A recent publication has generated debate on the response to child protection by services, as the authors have highlighted the necessity to impose a radical re-focus by using a holistic family approach as opposed to a child-centred one (Featherstone, White & Morris, 2014). Debate in the context of child protection is useful and enables policy-makers, researchers, and practitioners to seek out learning and to enhance, change, or consolidate society's response to this emotive topic. Stringent publicised evaluations continue to be necessary to support discussion and progress.

The therapeutic relationship

Rogers (1990) described the optimum relationship as therapeutic. This relationship is formed within a dyad of two people (a pairing): a learner who is sometimes referred to as 'a developing person' (for example, a parent) and a professional in the role of educator. Rogers identified six conditions which are necessary for the creation of this relationship. The following aspects interpret these six conditions in a context of early years.

1   A parent (service-user) and professional (service-provider) are in psychological contact.
2   The parent is vulnerable, has potentially poor physical and emotional health, and has mental instability.
3   The professional is demonstrating resilience by her or his capacity and ability to respond positively to professional responsibilities.
4   The professional shows respect and a non-judgemental response to the parent.
5   The professional is able to view the world from a parent's perspective and to communicate this understanding to the parent.
6   Optimum responsive care is the aim for all practitioners; however, Rogers recognised that any indication of empathy and positive regard contributes to creation of a therapeutic relationship.

Purpose

Trevithick (2003) had described one purpose of the therapeutic relationship as containing the negative emotions of a parent; therefore, during the learning process, a professional educator delivers informational *and* emotional support to a parent. Cooper (2004) commented that a therapeutic relationship had greater significance than the actual intervention, which indicates that the parent-professional relationship is an integral factor to supporting parents to change their actions and behaviour towards their children. The development of parenting skills does not automatically elevate a need to a context of child protection. Parents have always sought advice and guidance from keyworkers, health visitors, or teachers due to generic concerns about their child's social, physical, and emotional health. Humans have needs at different times of life, and seeking support is active parenting and a public demonstration of a parent's will to succeed in this most important role. Professionals have always sought information from parents and multi-disciplinary colleagues in order to respond to parental or professional concerns. An increase in confidence and self-esteem allows a parent to demonstrate latent skills and talents and allows a child to succeed.

56 *Child protection in the early years*

Outcome

Importance of the relationship was expressed by Howe (2008) as a medium in which an understanding of self was formed or potentially re-formed; therefore, the therapeutic relationship carries the intervention forward and also activates the transformation of knowledge into practice for the developing parent.

Value of a relationship

The concept of the parent-professional relationship having value was promoted by Trevithick (2003), who indicated that the quality of the relationship was linked to the knowledge and skills of each practitioner. Clear communication, consistency of practice, and inherent relational skills of practitioners have been identified by professionals and parents as contributing to a desirable skill set (Whitters, 2009).

Quality assurance

A lack of a quality-assurance system which considers the parent-professional relationship suggests a potential difficulty in evaluating inter-personal skills to a standard. A standard is sometimes promoted as principles of best practice by professionals. Rubin, Bukowski, and Parker (2006) suggested that the positive effect from a relationship could be defined in accordance with the emotions which were experienced by both parties. It seems that the value of a relationship is determined on an individual basis, based upon an emotional experience, and created within a context of principles of professional practice. These principles inform the **pedagogy** which affects the culture of each organisation.

Power within a relationship

Rogers recognised the first important step in the formation of a therapeutic relationship as a parent actively seeking support from a professional. This voluntary action creates an initial discussion point within the relationships which support the parents to develop an understanding of themselves and their personal circumstances. Every parent is keen to learn and recognises that an increase in parenting knowledge and skills can come from a variety of sources – for example, family, professionals in situ, media, and self.

If a parent who is involved in child protection processes actively seeks support, then it marks a pivotal point in safeguarding which commences a process of change. A voluntary referral, resulting in the parent accepting responsibility for dealing with negative issues, is differentiated from the mandatory referral which allocates an advisory role to a professional from an integrated team.

Interpretation and perceptions affect a parent's comprehension of his or her world in the form of **socially orientated beliefs** which are reflected in behaviour and actions. **Operational perspective** relates to the use of these beliefs to influence daily living – the way in which each person conducts his or her life. Power was identified by Cleaver and Freeman (1995) as being one social dimension of an operational perspective within the context of a parent-professional relationship. Power is transferred from professional to parent as the inner working model of the parent is re-configured through learning and development. The parents view their worlds differently – from their children's perspectives.

Power, in the form of knowledge and understanding which contributes to decision-making, cannot be transferred to a parent solely through imparting knowledge from educator to this primary carer. The parent has to be ready to learn, and a sensitive period for learning (Bowlby, 1979) can be supported through exploration of past experiences, particularly within childhood. It is important to note that professionals do not lose power of decision-making as a parent progresses through child protection processes. The relationship between parent and professional changes and may be termed a partnership as the two parties share the same goals, agree on processes, and identify signs of change and development. Knowledge and understanding give a parent power to contribute effectively to the process and may lead to the parent demonstrating the ability and capacity to respond to the child's needs, with minimum input from services.

Example from practice

When I commenced my career 30 years ago, practitioners were taught that adversity in childhood had a negative effect on the development of vulnerable parents. Parents were encourage 'to forget' the past and to look to the future. Practical activities were frequently used to facilitate this process within parenting workshops. Parents would record negative experiences and dramatically discard these recorded links to the past.

Currently, research has created a link between childhood experiences and the perceptions of adults, which has particular significance within a context of child protection. Van der Kolk (2003) identified that biology impacts upon a child's ability to perceive and integrate experiences. Structural and neurochemical changes contribute to the complexity of these circumstances, and the impact is sustained throughout our lifespans.

58 *Child protection in the early years*

> *Bob is a single parent who is caring for his young son and daughter. The children have recently been returned to their father from a year spent in accommodation. I meet Bob to deliver a parenting programme within the context of a child protection care plan. The intervention focuses upon attachment between child and primary carer, the family culture, supporting positive behaviour, and managing negative interactions. I feel that it is essential to facilitate Bob's understanding of self. This knowledge will enable me to deliver the programme in a way which responds to Bob's needs and his gaps in knowledge with regard to parenting. It will also support Bob to appreciate his inherent parenting skills and to gain confidence in the knowledge that change and development will build on his current expertise. Parents, in a child protection context, often do not have a realisation of their skills until a professional verbalises these attributes – the first step to raising self-esteem.*
>
> *Bob finds it easy to identify and describe negative experiences within his abusive childhood, and I encourage this vulnerable father to recall his emotions at that time. I ask Bob to consider who or what might have changed each experience and to share one happy memorable occasion. This leads Bob to clearly and vividly recount a few positive influences and memories from childhood, and the common feature is a secure attachment figure. Bob's interest in learning has been activated. His memories and subsequent evaluation of these experiences have provided this father with a base of knowledge to commence a sensitive period for learning and to embrace the intervention process. Bob's inner working model is starting to be re-configured. As the understanding of self develops, Bob will begin to view the world through the perspective of his children. He will be empowered to identify positive experiences for his son and daughter by exploring the negative examples from his own childhood.*

Ironically, if parenting skills develop in a context of child protection, then this may result in a disruption of the parent-professional relationship through a change of worker. When it is decided that a child can be removed from the child protection register, then another member of the team may replace the social worker during the six-week de-registration period. Following the six weeks de-registration, professionals from the health, education, and voluntary sectors will create working relationships with the parent and continue to provide support within this context. Early years' practitioners have daily contact with families and play an essential role in monitoring and sharing progress through this interim period and beyond. Self-sufficiency and independent decision-making may be challenging or even unachievable for parents without intensive support from services.

Bureaucracy

Circumstances of child protection may cause a range of emotions to be experienced and witnessed by a parent and professional. A relationship may change if both parties respond to one another's role signs and attempt to fulfil perceived expectations.

Example from practice

Research by Spratt and Callan (2004) had indicated that the use of particular interview rooms, in a context of child protection investigation, influenced parental behaviour. The rooms represented a negative environment to parents due to the association with previous child protection incidents. The parents' perceptions affected their actions and attitude.

Relationships may also be affected by the professional applying self-protective measures and by-passing the use of soft skills in order to implement policies and procedures in this emotive context.

Example from practice

I have made observations within core group meetings and Children's Panel in which the chair, as the spokesperson for the multi-disciplinary group, publicises decisions in an objective and factual manner to the parent and team. It is good professional conduct to adapt relational skills to suit these circumstances. Sharing decisions clearly and succinctly is essential during this stage of child protection processes. Discussion and interaction have been completed, and the objective is to promote clarity of understanding to the parent and integrated team in a context of bureaucracy; however, parents have expressed that the parent-professional relationship can be affected by the formality of circumstances.

Cleaver and Freeman (1995) suggested that professionals who were involved in a child protection case for a long period of time increased their tolerance to the existence of criteria in relation to application of formal procedures. Munro (2011) expressed a different view by indicating that evaluation and judgement were led by bureaucracy which restricted the application of professional expertise. Support and supervision of individuals and teams are essential to ensure that bureaucracy is used to guide assessment and decision-making based upon the expertise of multi-disciplinary professionals.

Levels of learning by professionals

Confidence and expertise in assessment and decision-making are related to levels of learning. The terms **basic** and **deep-level learning** can be applied to professionals. Workers may practice with a professional instinct and demonstrate **basic-level learning** by reacting to a parent's behaviour. Behaviour in the context of child protection is influenced by profound emotion. Parents usually experience and demonstrate a breadth of emotions and reactions: anger, aggression, disbelief, denial, rejection, confusion, fear, despair. The order is dependent on each parent's interpretation and perception of the circumstances, in addition to the influence from a professional response. Professional instinct does not necessarily involve **interpretation** of a parent's behaviour, which requires consideration of the mitigating factors.

The instinctive reaction can be transformed by practitioners reflecting upon and critically evaluating their parent-professional relationships. Peer observation and constructive feedback is an underutilised resource for professional development. This objective evaluation of practice can contribute to a pedagogy within an organisation which responds to the needs of a community by highlighting the abilities of the service-providers. Emotionally based reactions to vulnerability develop into empathic therapeutic interactions which are supported by understanding and the optimum application of knowledge with intent and purpose: **deep-level learning**.

Felt, expressed, and normative needs

Early intervention presupposes a need. **Felt need** is a parent's interpretation of personal need. This comprehension of need may differ from the professional's perspective, and it relates to the parent's understanding of self. It is through an understanding of oneself that a person interprets, comprehends, and reacts to circumstances.

> **Example from practice**
>
> *A parent may interpret need in a social, physical, or emotional context, on a personal basis or relative to a child. In my experience, parents do not tend to focus upon the emotional needs of children in a context of child protection. Parents' comprehension of need often relates to practical issues with definitive outcomes – for example, the cleanliness*

Child protection in the early years 61

of a house, care routines for children, weaning and healthy diets, rehabilitation from addiction, anger management, and budgeting for daily living.

Expressed need is a parent's verbal or written display of need. The expectation of a professional response may affect this behaviour. Formal systems, in which a parent is invited to contribute, facilitate direct signalling of need by the parent – for example, core group meetings initiated by the social work team, and panel meetings with the Children's Reporter (Scottish Children's Reporter Administration, 2009; Scottish Government, 2010). Formal systems of recorded communications are Integrated Assessment Forms, the Graded Care Profile, and child protection plans (Polnay & Scrivastava, 1995; Scottish Executive, 2005).

Need can also be expressed indirectly by a parent. Child protection training and support in the field should enable practitioners to understand and respond to these cues from vulnerable parents.

Example from practice

A practice example of indirect signalling of need relates to a parent presenting at Accident and Emergency with injuries pertinent to domestic violence. An integral part of child protection training is teaching professionals to be observant for signs of abuse in adult primary carers in addition to children. Parents may wear clothing which does not hide abusive marks in the expectation that 'someone will notice.' Alternatively, parents may choose clothing in order to hide abuse, and this can alert a vigilant worker if the clothing is unusual for a particular parent or inappropriate to the weather or time of day.

Finally, **normative need** is interpretation of the needs of a parent and child which are assessed against professional standards. The standards relate to the context of a professional discipline – for example, health, education, or social work. These professional assessments of need, in a context of child protection, are based upon evidence of parents' failure to achieve conditions which are necessary to support the health and wellbeing of a child. A need demonstrates that these conditions are not being met.

Informal verbal communication

The regular use of informal verbal communication provides parents with a medium in which to directly or indirectly seek support. Katz, La Placa, and Hunter (2007) reported that parental control within support systems was a key factor to engagement. Communication gives parents control of access to services.

Small settings, which Lupyan and Dale (2010) describe as **esoteric**, develop a communication system in response to learning constraints and to the unique communicative needs of parents and professionals. For example, vulnerable parents and an integrated team may have universal knowledge and interest in issues relating to addiction, mental health, and child protection, which creates a specific focus upon their system of communication from the local culture.

Dressler (2004) identified culture as the basis of a community's interactive systems, and he applied the term **cultural consonance** to describe the beliefs and behaviours of a community. The use of informal verbal communication between parents and professionals demonstrates **a social collective function** (Cargile, Giles, Ryan & Bradac, 1994) within an organisation.

Optimal communication in a service

Cuthbert, Rayns, and Stanley (2011) identified that the optimum entry point was realised by any service which administered support at the initial point of contact or sign-posted a service-user to other agencies. Social interaction between parents and professionals (for example, informal chatting during drop-off and pick-up periods) has two interdependent features which relate to a parent's declaration of need and an expectation of support from the professional (Trappes-Lomax, 2004). This phenomenon in which a parent signals and a professional recognises the help-seeking cues represents the **optimal communication system** within services (Brighton, Smith & Kirby, 2005).

Practitioners will respond empathically by listening to the parent's description of adversities. This commences the process towards an increase in a parent's comprehension of self which creates a strong foundation for learning and change. Professionals may not have the appropriate experience or be qualified to respond to a parent's needs, but a common and effective approach is sign-posting between multi-disciplinary members of an integrated team. Research has shown that a positive relationship with one professional can be used to forge relationships between service-users and the extended team (Whitters, 2015). A parent's engagement with one establishment should be harnessed by professionals to encourage links to a broader support system. The communicative strategies and positive parent-professional relationships are **connectors** in this chain of events within a setting.

This use of the medium of the parent-professional relationship to transfer a positive influence from one microsystem to another (Bronfenbrenner, 1979, 2005) indicates **strength in the organisational capacity** of the dyad.

The relationship creates **a meso-system**, a bridge between two micro-systems. The meso-system incorporates transference of knowledge and attitude – for example, positivity. The positive aspects of a strong relationship, which is created in a pre-crisis voluntary period of engagement, can be transferred during implementation of mandatory child protection procedures. This transferability of positivity to a relationship which is subject to influences from a different ecological system is another indication of strength in the organisational capacity of the pairing between service-user and service-provider.

Demand characteristics

Theory can be used to gain comprehension of verbal interaction within a parent-professional relationship. The Social-Address Model by Magnusson and Stattin (2006) promotes understanding of the dynamics and fluctuating circumstances of relationships between service-providers and service-users. Practitioners will recognise the application of the term **demand characteristics**, which is demonstrated by a parent attempting to gain power in the relationship for parental needs, as opposed to needs of the vulnerable child. Demand characteristics (for example, verbal interaction) create a joint focus of attention between two parties – parent and professional. Practitioners develop expertise in responding to parents who communicate frequently and seek professional attention on a daily basis, in addition to parents who are reticent and require encouragement to instigate interaction. Both approaches to communication can hide or reveal a need within a vulnerable family.

A parent can reject verbal overtures and apply a buffering mechanism – for example, withdrawing eye-contact. This can impose negativity or halt the interaction with a professional. Magnusson and Stattin described this effect as having **negative social stimulus value**. The potential to apply a buffering mechanism suggests that demand characteristics may be generative (positive) or disruptive (negative) within a context in which need is exposed and support is sought.

Peripheral participation in a service

Lave and Wenger (1991) described the process in which a new parent internalised a socio-culture of practice as **peripheral participation**. Social relationships between parents within organisations are encouraged in order to promote inclusion for newcomers and to facilitate integration into the learning environment; therefore, relationships between new and established parents support engagement with services. Most organisations promote these social interactions, and environmental factors can contribute to positive relationships developing between service-users. For example, attractive adult seating and a water outlet within a nursery children's cloakroom or school reception represent an interactive area and give implicit permission to stay. A pictorial and text information board which is clearly targeted to parents can provide a focus for discussion between families. Research on the Headstart programmes found that a source of heat, light, and food encouraged service-users to socialise and integrate into the culture of an organisation (Lamb-Parker et al., 2001).

The research findings by Crittenden (1985) suggested that vulnerable adults gravitate toward individuals with similar internal working models in order to access help. It is often observed that parents will create peer relationships which are based upon a common shared need. Emotional and informational support is difficult to give to a peer from a perspective of personal vulnerability. Practitioners develop an acute awareness of the positive or negative impact one vulnerable family may have upon another. It is important that teams share this information on the local socio-cultural practices within an organisation and respond.

Example from practice

During my career I often spend time in waiting areas of services, health, education, or social work, prior to attending case conferences. I observe parents waiting to have a supervised access visit with their children who live in kinship or foster care. Anxiety and anticipation is obvious and palpable at times as parents wait for the conditions of access to be achieved in order to see their children. Parents are waiting for a family room to be free, for the supervision support staff to be available, for the reception clock to indicate that the visiting time is about to commence, for permission to resume the parenting role, albeit for a two-hour period. Apprehensive parents will seek support in the immediate environment. I notice groups of parents creating instant friendships; recognising the shared context; discussing the trappings to these access visits (bags of toys, snack or lunch, changes of clothes for the children); and seeking approval for the choice of presents which have been bought to demonstrate positive parenting.

Perceptions

Each person interprets his or her world in a unique way, and **perceptions are the operating principles** which determine behaviour of individuals or organisations. Operational perspectives are affected and modified by human interaction; therefore, perceptions can alter over time. **Learning** leads to parents interpreting and interacting with their world from new perspectives. **Development** results in parents identifying and responding to their children's needs and fulfilling societal expectations in a context of child protection.

The parent-professional relationship provides a means for service-users and service-providers to acknowledge one another's perceptions and to create a base of understanding which supports a period of learning. As a parent's interpretation of his or her world alters, the inner working model is reformed and ultimately affects actions and behaviour, which is a prime consideration in child protection.

Research (Whitters, 2015) has indicated similarities and differences in the perceptions of parents and the professionals which relate to social, emotional, and cultural influences. Positive outcomes from early intervention are linked to **convergence** of professional and parental perceptions. **Divergence** in the perceptions of parents and professionals indicates that optimum conditions to support a positive outcome have not been realised.

Child protection – positive perception

Lave and Wenger (1991) had described the process by which human beings integrate into a community by internalising a culture of practice. This can result in normalisation of child protection within a locality. It is related to a family's immersion in a particular organisation and community. Magnusson and Stattin (2006) linked life events to changes in a human's internal frame of reference, and daily interactions in a community (in addition to specific events) expose parents to potential influences. The micro-system of human development (Bronfenbrenner, 1979) is composed of features which relate to daily living – for example, health, education, and social services as well as the shopping area and local environs. The micro-system also encompasses relationships with family and professionals as well as transient encounters within a local community. Members of a community may spend significant periods of time each day in their locality. A shopping centre is often regarded as a focal point to wait, meet, interact, and transact.

Example from practice

June takes her daughter to nursery and drops her off quickly in order to collect her methadone prescription from the chemist – her 'daily script.' Addiction management is structured by professionals, and June has to attend the pharmacy by 9.15 am. The appointment system puts pressure on this mother as she takes her son to school for 9.00 am and her daughter to nursery for 9.15 am. The nursery reception staff will not allow early access to the building. June could change the timing of these arrangements, but her rehabilitation is encompassed within child protection procedures, and she has not realised that implementation of the care plan can be negotiated. The first few hours of every day are predictably stressful for June. After taking her methadone, June stands outside the chemist with other local people who are also participating in a 'meths-programme' at the same time each day. These vulnerable individuals sit on the seats within the shopping centre precinct and observe their world; uniformed professionals accompany mothers and fathers for supervised access visits – going to the shops with their children to practise creating patterns of daily living which encompass positive parenting skills; a queue of men and women, old and young, has formed outside the pharmacy to access their scripts; the local co-op has a large poster on the front door – the Children's Charter, which proclaims clearly to the public that child protection is everyone's responsibility; a group of teenagers have skipped school, and they are reading a Child-Line poster on the window of the bakery; a council escort jumps out of a marked car and lifts a little baby from a car seat. This community has many visual reminders of child protection which are apparent every day and contribute to normalising the concept.

Child protection – negative perception

The negative perception of child protection by professionals can be linked to physical and emotional harm to children, and the forensic investigative processes. Professionals have formal and informal influences to the development of their attitudes – for example, undergraduate training in a specific discipline, and peer modelling by any multi-disciplinary worker. Howe (2013) had recorded that a professional's ability to empathise with a client might require suppression of a personal viewpoint or belief; therefore, this is also an important area of professional development.

Example from practice

A child is accommodated straight from the Children's Panel meeting. The multi-disciplinary professionals re-group in the street outside the building of the Children's Reporter, which is situated in the city centre. The workers stand close together as the fresh air returns their thoughts to the outside world. During child protection meetings, the world exists within the microcosm of a room. Shoppers walk past, laughing and carefree in the spring sunshine and swinging their bags of purchases. Every professional agreed with the decision, every professional is relieved that the child is safe, but I am sure that every practitioner, regardless of the discipline, experienced a sense of professional and personal failure at this point in child protection processes. This is a common reaction. Our job is to improve the birth family's capacity and ability to care for a child, but accommodation definitively shows that the projected outcome has not been achieved. At the point of accommodation, professionals' positive and negative emotions are juxtaposed. Professionals re-visit care plans and implementation of intervention; they discuss 'if only I had . . .' scenarios. Prior to an imminent period of accommodation, the necessity to protect a child provides clarity and focus to workers. If the expectation of a Children's Panel decision is fulfilled, then the relief which professionals feel can be overwhelming; however, once the child is safe from harm, then professional reflection has to be managed and supported by a member of the team who has objectivity. Objectivity inserts realism and sense, and it supports professionals to look forward and to prepare for the next task.

Negative relationships between parents and professionals do occur. The formal context presents parents with the right to request a change in the parent-professional dyad, and this may be upheld.

Example from practice

The professional and parent should discuss the issues. Relationships cannot always be changed in this context. Requesting a change of worker is often an emotional reaction from a parent to the circumstances. Parents should be encouraged to change the circumstances instead and to put their emotional energy into development of parenting skills in order to achieve the expectations of the child protection processes.

A positive relationship with one professional can be used to create a relationship with another member of the integrated team. A relationship can also be applied as a mediation tool to change a negative perception of a relationship with another provider. Practice associated with this strategy can be a joint home-visit or meeting within a service in which continuity of the care plan and parental and professional roles are clarified. Expectations should be clear.

Personalities

Personality influences any human relationship. 'Approachable' and 'honest' are terms used by parents regarding personal attributes which contribute to a positive relationship between professional and parent (Whitters, 2009).

Example from practice

Parents and professionals agree that the absence of positive characteristics has a negative influence upon their relationships. This suggests that a proactive approach by planned demonstration of positive personal characteristics is deemed to be desirable in the creation of an effective parent-professional relationship. Colleagues often share practice strategies with one another and role-model positive relationship-building with parents.

Relationships develop over time; therefore, strategies need to be adjusted in response to a parent's stage of learning and development. Munro (2011) expressed that not all techniques and skills which were applied by professionals were recordable – for example, intuition was independent of language, but the potential impact upon the relationship was high.

It is important that each practitioner recognises his or her unique contribution to relationship-building with vulnerable families. The combination of knowledge, understanding, and personality supports a demonstration of empathy within a therapeutic relationship. The final chapter focuses upon the implementation gap and pedagogy of each organisation.

References

Bowlby, J. (1979). *The making and breaking of affectional bonds.* Abingdon: Routledge.

Brighton, H., Smith, K., & Kirby, S. (2005). Review: Language as an evolutionary system. *Journal of Physics of Life Reviews, volume 2.* Retrieved May 2012, from www.sciencedirect.com

Bronfenbrenner, U. (1979). *The ecology of human development* (2nd ed.). Cambridge: Harvard University Press.

Bronfenbrenner, U. (2005). *Making human beings human.* Thousand Oaks, CA: Sage.

Care Sector Consortium. (1997). *National occupational standards for early years care and education NVQ/SVQ level 3.* London: Local Government Management Board.

Cargile, A. C., Giles, H., Ryan, E. B., & Bradac, J. J. (1994). Language attitudes as a social process: A conceptual model and new directions. *Language and Communication, volume 14, number 3.* London: Elsevier Science Ltd.

Central Advisory Council for Education. (1967). *Children and their primary schools ('the plowden report').* London: HMSO.

Cleaver, H., & Freeman, P. (1995). *Parental perspectives in cases of suspected child abuse.* London: Her Majesty's Stationery Office.

Cooper, M. (2004). Towards a relationally-orientated approach to therapy: Empirical support and analysis. *British Journal of Guidance and Counselling, volume 32, number 4,* 451–460. Retrieved August 2012, from http://strathprints.strath.ac.uk

Crittenden, P. M. (1985). Social networks, quality of child rearing, and child development. *Journal of Child Development, volume 56, number 5*. Retrieved March 2012, from www.jstor.org/stable/1130245

Cuthbert, C., Rayns, G., & Stanley, K. (2011). *All babies count, prevention and protection for vulnerable babies*. London: National Society for the Prevention of Cruelty to Children.

Daniel, B., Burgess, C., & Scott, J. (2012). *Review of child neglect in Scotland*. Edinburgh: Scottish Government.

Department for Children, Schools and Families. (2009). *Common assessment framework*. Retrieved March 11, 2009, from www.dcsf.gov.uk/everychildmatters/strategy/deliveringservices1/caf/cafframework

Department of Health. (1995). *Child protection: Messages from research*. London: HMSO.

Dressler, W. W. (2004). Culture and the risk of disease. *British Medical Bulletin, volume 69*, 21–39. Retrieved June 2012, from http://oxfordjournals.org

Edelman, L. (2004). *A relationship-based approach to early intervention*. Retrieved December 2013, from www.cde.state.co.us/earlychildhoodconnections/Technical.htm

Featherstone, B., White, S., & Morris, K. (2014). *Re-imagining child protection: Towards humane social work with families*. London: Policy Press.

Howe, D. (2008). Relationship-based thinking and practice in social work. *Journal of Social Work Practice: Psychoanalytic Approaches in Health, Welfare and the Community, volume 22, 45–56*. London: Routledge.

Howe, D. (2013). *Empathy, what it is and why it matters*. Basingstoke: Palgrave Macmillan.

Katz, I., La Placa, V., & Hunter, S. (2007). *Barriers to inclusion and successful engagement of parents in mainstream services*. York: Joseph Rowntree Foundation.

Lamb-Parker, F., Piotrkowski, C. S., Baker, A. J. L., Kessler-Sklar, S., Clark, B., & Peay, L. (2001). Understanding barriers to parent involvement in Head Start: A research-community partnership. *Early Childhood Research Quarterly, volume 16*. Retrieved October 2009, from www.elsevierdirect.com

Lave, J., & Wenger, E. (1991). *Situated learning, legitimate peripheral participation*. Cambridge: Cambridge University Press.

Lupyan, G., & Dale, R. (2010). Language structure is partly determined by social structure. *Journal PLoS One, volume 5, number 1*. Retrieved May 2012, from www.plosone.org

Magnusson, D., & Stattin, H. (2006). The person in context: A holistic-interactionist approach. In W. Damon & R. Lerner (Eds.), *Handbook of Child Psychology, volume 1*. Hoboken, NJ: John Wiley & Sons.

Moran, P., Ghate, D., & van der Merwe, A. (2004). *What works in parenting support? A review of the international evidence*. London: HMSO.

Moullin, S., Waldfogel, J., & Washbrook, E. (2014). *Baby bonds – parenting, attachment and a secure base for children*. London: The Sutton Trust.

Munro, E. (2011). *The Munro review of child protection: Final report, a child-centred system*. London: Information Policy Team.

Parton, N. (2007). Safeguarding children: A socio-historical analysis. In K. Wilson & A. James (Eds.), *The child protection handbook*. London: Balliere Tindall Elsevier.

Polnay, L., & Scrivastava, O. P. (1995). *Graded care profile scale*. Glasgow: Child Protection Team, Centenary House.

Rogers, C. (1990). *The Carl Rogers reader*. Cornwall: MPG Books Ltd.

Rubin, K. H., Bukowski, W. M., & Parker, J. G. (2006). Peer interactions, relationships and groups. In W. Damon & R. M. Lerner (Eds.), *Handbook of child psychology, volume 3* (pp. 576–580). Hoboken, NJ: John Wiley & Sons.

Scottish Children's Reporter Administration. (2009). *Children under two years referred to the children's reporter*. Stirling: SCRA.

Scottish Executive. (1997). *The children (Scotland) act 1995*. Norwich: The Stationery Office.

Scottish Executive. (2005). *Integrated assessment for Glasgow's children*. (Appendix 1, pp. 1–9, 12–13). Retrieved April 18, 2005, from S:\CCS\2003-05\Integrated AssessmentFramework\IAF-FinalDraft.doc

Scottish Government. (2008). *A guide to getting it right for every child*. Edinburgh: Scottish Government.

Scottish Government. (2010). *National guidance for child protection in Scotland*. Edinburgh: Scottish Government.

Scottish Government. (2012). *National parenting strategy, making a positive difference to children and young people through parenting*. Edinburgh: Scottish Government.

Scottish Government. (2014a). *National guidance for child protection in Scotland 2014*. Edinburgh: Scottish Government.

Scottish Government. (2014b). *Children and young people (Scotland) Act. (2014)*. Edinburgh: Scottish Government.

Scottish Government. (2015). *Family nurse partnership national report 2014–2015*. Retrieved February 2016, from www.gov.scot/Topics/People/Young-People/early-years/parenting-early-learning

Spratt, T., & Callan, J. (2004). Parents' views on social work interventions in child welfare cases. *British Journal of Social Work, volume 34*, 199–224. Oxford: Oxford University Press.

Sudbery, J. (2010). Key features of therapeutic social work: The use of relationship. *Journal of Social Work Practice: Psychotherapeutic Approaches in Health, Welfare and the Community, volume 16, 149–162*. London: Routledge.

Trappes-Lomax, H. (2004). Discourse analysis. In A. Davies & C. Elder (Eds.), *The handbook of applied linguistics* (pp. 133–146). Oxford: Blackwell Publishing Ltd.

Trevithick, P. (2003). Effective relationship-based practice: A theoretical exploration. *Journal of Social Work Practice, volume 17, number 2*. Oxford: Oxford University Press.

United Nations Convention on the Rights of the Child (UNCRC). (1989). *United nations convention on the rights of the child*. Geneva: UNCRC.

United Nations General Assembly. (1989). *United Nations convention on the rights of the child (UNCRC)*. Geneva: Office of the United Nations High Commissioner for Human Rights (OHCHR).

Van der Kolk, B. (2003). *The neurobiology of childhood trauma and abuse.* Retrieved May 2016, from www.researchgate.net/publications/10779024

Whitters, H. G. (2009). *Parents and an integrated team: Developing and maintaining effective relationships to support early interventions.* Published MSc thesis. Glasgow: Strathclyde University Library.

Whitters, H. G. (2015). *Perceptions of the influences upon the parent-professional relationship in a context of early intervention and child protection.* Published doctoral thesis. Retrieved January 2016, from http://ethos.bl.uk/OrderDetails.do?uin=uk.bl.ethos.655502

4 Pedagogy and the implementation gap

The concept of an implementation gap indicates a potential weakness in the links between research, legislation, and practice in the workplace. Research has shown that effective implementation of a curriculum responds to cultural and personal needs of children, within each family and local community. Support and supervision are regulated processes which contribute to maintaining standards of practice at the local and national levels, and they enable the practitioner to understand the transference of research findings to daily work; however, developing pedagogy which adheres to regulations and responds to local need is challenging.

Reflective practice

'Reflective practice' is a term which has become popular within the past few years in the context of professional development, but practitioners often ask:

'What is reflective practice?'
'Can it be taught?'
'Is it planned or spontaneous?'
'Do you have to be experienced in order to constructively criticise your own practice?'
'How do you criticise the practice of colleagues?'

Reflective practice is not a new concept. Practitioners over the past few decades have been encouraged to: 'Think about your actions, evaluate your practice, learn from one another, plan, do, and review.' Learning and development evolve throughout our careers, and reflective learning usually occurs informally, but workplaces may also necessitate a formal format of recorded review and development. Professional reflection may take place within each working day, once a month, or perhaps during in-service training throughout the year. Staff often comment that reflection takes place on their journeys to and from work as the brain processes and sorts the day's events.

Inner working model

Reflective practice involves a professional consolidating or re-defining his or her inner working model as described by Bowlby (1979). The inner working model represents each person's interpretation and understanding of the world. A multitude of information is retained throughout our lifespans. Each experience is used to re-asses information already stored and to enhance comprehension which ultimately affects behavioural responses through reactions or interactions with the world. Our knowledge, understanding, and skills increase over time.

Relationship-based practice is most effective if the practitioner acknowledges and responds to a child and parent's interpretation of his or her world. These perspectives are necessary bases with which to commence a process of development. Each practitioner will retain information on families and create links through discussion with other professionals, which contributes to understanding. Listening, in addition to talking with parents, provides a rich context for professional learning. Parents will share information and interpretation from a personal context and will demonstrate behaviour which is associated with their perceptions and relationships in family and community. This means that communicative strategies and interventions can be adapted to suit the needs of families and, additionally, to respond to the way in which a family leads its life. It is known that the earliest relational experiences provide a blueprint for subsequent relationships; therefore, the experience of relationships between a child, parent, and professional, and the accompanying actions and behaviour, will influence relationships within and outside the family network.

Four sources of knowledge

The outcome of reflection is expertise, and it is useful to consider sources of information which may enhance your knowledge, understanding, and skills. There are four sources of knowledge which can support a practitioner to reflect and to understand practice.

1   Documentation in the form of policy, guidance, and theory
2   Observing, interacting, and learning from professional peers
3   Observing, interacting, and listening to children
4   Observing, interacting, and listening to parents.

Pedagogy and the implementation gap 75

1 POLICY, GUIDANCE, AND THEORY

Policy identifies optimum outcomes which are based upon research concerning the needs and rights of children and parents and are set within national or international frameworks.

Guidance promotes generic ideas and suggestions for supporting children and their parents to achieve these outcomes.

Theory supports understanding of practice. Theory facilitates the practitioner to investigate the component aspects of a concept, to identify the original ideas and experiences which contribute to the creation of concepts, and to use this information to gain meaning from practice. An increase in comprehension responds to practitioner's questions on pedagogy, choice and implementation of interventions, and the link to outcomes. Understanding which is gained from theory enhances practice by clarifying the role and responsibilities of workers from multi-disciplines which gives purpose to our actions and responses to service-users.

2 OBSERVING, INTERACTING, AND LEARNING FROM PROFESSIONAL PEERS

Scenarios and case studies from a wide range of organisations are often used in guidance material; however, optimum practice should reflect the culture of an organisation or family, often termed **cultural sensitivity**. The culture of each organisation is determined by the needs of the service-users, adversities and the protective factors in the local community, and the ethos of each establishment. This knowledge is relevant to service-providers in the delivery of services within each setting. Most workplaces impose a mentoring system for new workers in which experienced practitioners show newcomers how to implement policies into practice by demonstrating or expressing formal and informal do's and don'ts of the organisation. These examples of practice are often implicitly or explicitly promoted as the standard which a new member of the team should be striving to attain.

Social referencing is an example of this process of learning which occurs when professionals experience the culture of an organisation through spontaneous or planned observations of colleagues. It is known that work teams create a system of beliefs, principles, and values over a period of time by using social referencing, and this shared understanding is represented by the pedagogy of an establishment.

Multi-disciplinary teams are composed of professionals who are trained in different disciplines but operate as an integrated group – for example, health, education, social work, housing, police, and the voluntary sector. Workers will often practice together. For example, within home visits, the context of joint-working promotes learning from one practitioner to another.

76 *Pedagogy and the implementation gap*

During core groups, child protection reviews, or inter-agency conferences, professionals and parents will sit around a table to discuss a family's needs and the responses from services. Practitioners will recognise the tense atmosphere that can occur within these meetings as professionals focus upon the speaker and parent, watching, listening, and role-modelling. This context provides many formal and informal opportunities for learning through social referencing which determines aspects of practice relating to leadership styles, practice priorities, communication techniques, use of sympathy or empathy, and team cohesion or dissipation.

3 OBSERVING, INTERACTING, AND LISTENING TO CHILDREN

Practitioners are already familiar with the daily use of observations of children in their care to assess each child's developmental level and, consequently, areas of need and strengths. Evaluating how children interact with a setting informs planning for the content of lessons and presentation of a rich and stimulating learning environment.

However, practitioners should also take time to focus specifically upon children's relationships by observing their reactions and interactions with peers and with adults who may be primary or secondary carers. Primary carers are usually parents or extended family, and secondary carers are professionals. This source of learning is invaluable for comprehending the creation, maintenance, and fluctuating nature of relationships for each child.

4 OBSERVING, INTERACTING, AND LISTENING TO PARENTS

Observing, interacting, and listening to parents also offers the worker an insight into relationships within a particular organisation, family, and community. There are many opportunities to observe interactions which occur on a daily basis – for example, in the playground at drop-off and pick-up, and informal meeting and greeting. Dyads (pairings) are formed during parent-child or parent-practitioner interactions, parent-parent conversations, and parent-peer communications.

Pedagogy

Each organisation has a pedagogy which refers to the implementation of the service by the workforce. The creation and implementation of a play environment is a prime area in which the skill of the early years' practitioner can support or hinder development of a child. Every environment is interpreted by a child as a place to explore in a context of play. Exploratory play is instinctive. Practitioners are faced with many challenges in relation

Pedagogy and the implementation gap 77

to planning and setting up a playroom due to the requirements which have to be considered:

- Legislation and requirements from inspectorate and local authority
- Curriculum
- National and local practice models
- Early years' themes (long, medium, and short term) which encompass topics and cultural celebrations
- Each child's interests
- Interests of peer groups
- Each child's long-term and short-term family circumstances
- Each child's long-term or short-term additional support for learning needs.

Presenting evidence of planning is a requirement for inspection. About 20 years ago, nursery nurses would *forward plan* and set up an environment in relation to expected learning outcomes for groups of children and offer a wide variety of planned experiences which provided opportunities for development in every aspect. Currently, early years' practitioners will *forward plan* a generic environment which provides a broad range of experiential opportunities and incorporates choices to support each child's decision-making. Responding to individual needs and circumstances occurs during interaction between the attachment figure / keyworker and child. Generally, playroom staff operate as a close supportive team, and children may have several attachment figures.

A child has the capacity and ability to learn in any environment if a practitioner provides emotional support which results in a child seeking out learning, making decisions, retaining and using knowledge, and practising his or her skills to achieve comprehension of his or her world. The material environment of a playroom provides an exploratory base for rich learning to occur. The catalyst is the partnership of child and practitioner which is based upon a therapeutic relationship.

An effective pedagogy should take into account the strengths and weaknesses of service-users in a community, and delivery of support should reflect the skills within an organisation. Team members require generic skills which relate to the core functioning of the group, but each practitioner has a specialist skill or personal attribute which can contribute to effective and potentially innovative pedagogy. Work teams which recognise input from individuals, and the whole group, are most effective in the early years' context. Teams evolve over time, and optimum output is influenced by consideration of strategy and operational practices, expertise of individuals, consistency of performance by a team, and the resilience of the workforce who practise in the context of child protection.

Implementation gap

It is essential that research is used to inform practice, but it can be challenging for practitioners to transfer knowledge, which is presented in an academic context, to enhance comprehension of daily work. Senior staff have a responsibility to seek out this source of learning and to share with teams in a medium which is appropriate to practice. Line managers should develop an awareness of the learning needs and learning styles of workers and present information accordingly. Theory and practice are complementary sources of learning in the field. Registration has resulted in senior staff being educated to degree level. This process has been effective in creating productive links between researchers, research, practitioners, and practice.

Generic courses which are delivered by a local authority are useful and necessary, but gaining skills associated with implementation in each workplace is integral to best practice. It is important that practitioners have the opportunity to apply this increase in knowledge and understanding. Any generic courses should always be reviewed by the team in the context of an organisational pedagogy, culture of the community, needs and strengths of families, and the abilities of the workers.

Katz, La Placa, and Hunter (2007) had focused upon positive role-modelling in a review on barriers to parental engagement. These authors indicated that a service-provider could only create an effective relationship with a service-user if a professional culture of trust was apparent within the organisation. Positive influences from role-modelling in the parent-professional dyad are dependent on circumstances which occur within two systems of human development:

1   The pedagogy of an organisation which is influenced from the **macrosystem** in the form of policy and leadership strategies.
2   The pedagogy of an organisation which is influenced from the **microsystem** in the context of daily practice.

Pedagogy and child protection

It is well-known that vulnerable families will transfer between similar services within or beyond their local area until engagement occurs with a team of service-providers. Parents often describe an organisational ethos which is linked to each setting. A culture of practice which reflects the same principles and values by each service-provider evolves within an integrated team (Lord, Kinder, Wilkin, Atkinson & Harland, 2008). Timely responses, availability of professional support, and a friendly manner are promoted by parents and professionals as conducive to a positive relationship. Professionals may express that logistically there are difficulties in responding at the point that a parent signals need; however, effective responses can be momentary and include sign-posting if applicable. Acknowledging need by thanking a parent for sharing personal information, respectfully verbalising the parent's emotions, and making definitive arrangements for future discussion takes minutes of professional time and has an invaluable impact upon the parent-professional relationship.

A parent-professional relationship should not encompass punitive measures. Legal repercussions in response to a crime associated with child protection will be decided and administered in court. Practice managers who oversee child protection procedures in the field may impose consequences if a care plan has not been followed by a parent. Managers in child protection are chosen for expertise which includes excellent diplomacy and an understanding of the use of professional and personal skills. An effective practice strategy which I have often observed is reference to the judicial system or local authority policy as the rationale for decisions. This clearly promotes the formality of the professional role with regard to implementation of policies and procedures. Child protection decisions are not based upon the personal opinion of a worker, and this point should always be communicated to a parent and recorded in meeting minutes.

The dyad of service-user and service-provider is a pairing of two people within the roles of parent and practitioner. The dyad can be regarded as a mini-team who are working together to achieve the same outcome. If the parent and professional agree on the outcome and processes to achieve set goals, then this mini-team can function efficiently and productively; however, there may be disagreement between the two parties which ultimately will impact upon the performance from the team (Whitters, 2015, 2016).

Divergence of perceptions

The perceptions of individuals is a key concept which affects actions, behaviour, and emotions. Formation of perceptions is linked to personal, social, and cultural influences within a community and organisation. Divergence of perceptions can create a potential weakness in the organisational capacity of the parent-professional dyad (pairing) – therefore affecting the implementation of intervention. Several implications for practice can be identified:

- There may be a difference in the knowledge, understanding, and expectations of parents and professionals in relation to child protection processes, roles and responsibilities, and associative outcomes. This could potentially affect the agreement of goals, recognition of progress, engagement of parents with services, and ultimately the creation of an equal parent-professional partnership.
- Professionals may not be aware of this divergence or recognise changes in the perceptions of parents; therefore, early interventional strategies may not be implemented in response to reconstruction of the inner working model of each parent as learning and development occur.
- A difference in perceptions may affect the practitioner's demonstration of empathic responding to the parent and reduce the impact of this necessary condition to the creation of a therapeutic alliance.

Convergence of perceptions

Convergence of perceptions can create potential strength in the organisational capacity of the parent-professional dyad – therefore contributing to effective implementation of early intervention. Several implications for practice can be identified:

- Parents and professionals may have the same knowledge, understanding, and expectations associated with communication in an organisation – therefore contributing to a system which supports parents to be active participants in a process of change and development. This leads to a positive relationship and potentially to implementation of intervention in the pre-crisis period.
- The creation of an effective communication system which responds to local cultural influences may be supported by the ethos of an organisation and by knowledge and understanding of a team in addition to management and timely deployment of personnel – therefore utilising characteristics pertinent to an organisation in order to benefit parents and to facilitate the role of professional.

Pedagogy is influenced by local and national practice models. The next section describes potential applications to daily work in health, education, and social work in a context of Scottish guidance, but the rationale can easily be applied to other practice models (Department for Children, Schools and Families, 2009; Scottish Government, 2008).

Example from practice

The tools of Scotland's National Practice Model are accessed by services to support representation and comprehension of the child's world. The My World Triangle depicts a child's wants, needs, and interests. Use of principles from the Shanarri Wellbeing wheel is the action plan which publicises the input from services and family to keep a child safe, healthy, achieving, nurtured, active, respected, responsible, and included. Finally, the Resilience Matrix is used to record and to understand the influences from adversities and protective factors upon a child's vulnerability, resilience, and wellbeing.

Positive and negative perceptions of a parent can be recorded within protective factors or adversities in the matrix – for example, agreement or disagreement that a parent's addiction is an adversity to a child's development, agreement or disagreement that contact with a family member has a negative impact upon a child's emotions, agreement or disagreement that a parent has engaged with services, and agreement or disagreement that a child should be placed on the child protection register. These are common contentious issues between professionals and parents.

Recording parental perceptions informs the integrated team of influences which are affecting this primary carer's actions and behaviour. It provides a focus for discussion with a parent during implementation of action plans, and importantly it is also a way of recording and acknowledging positive change. Core groups, Children's Panel, and legal representatives seek evidence of change in order to inform decision-making. Long-term goals can appear to be unachievable to vulnerable parents, but using the matrix to record little positive changes and to demonstrate the resultant impact upon a child is a simple, effective practice technique. A vulnerable parent can gain hope and expectation through recorded recognition of progress.

Practitioners may not realise the amount and relevance of information which they accumulate through observation in the workplace or community (Department for Children, Schools and Families, 2010; Scottish Government, 2012). During training sessions, I often ask participants to give a list of the ways in which parents signal or reveal need, and practitioners give the following examples of cues:

- Body language and personal presentation
- Verbal interaction or little communication
- Attendance on time or earlier or later than required
- Non-attendance

82 Pedagogy and the implementation gap

- A change of peer friendships in the service or observed within the community
- Change in common daily conduct or habits.

It is important that practitioners are aware of the implications of this information as applied to each parent in an organisation. This knowledge and understanding can be achieved through daily discussion with colleagues. A few minutes spent reviewing a parent's presentation and interaction with the service, on that day, are invaluable to applying information on the sociocultural aspects of vulnerable families. Direct or indirect signalling of need can be detected by discussion of a parent's behaviour with multi-disciplinary colleagues. Timely responses can be made. Senior staff have a responsibility to lead the workforce in increasing comprehension of the world from a parent's perspective in order to protect children.

Chronological records should be used by every member of a team to retain this information and prompt discussion by professionals. A communication diary can be used to alert the playroom team that a chronological record has been recorded, and it should be reviewed and discussed by seniors and keyworkers. Consistency of practice is key to positive outcomes. Minor incidents or observations within chronological records can gain significance due to accumulation and comparison of information over time. Electronic records can be shared easily with every member of an extended team and ensure that information is interpreted by professionals from different disciplines. At induction to a service, parents give informed consent for sharing information between service-providers. The perception of one professional may differ from another due to the context of a discipline – for example, health, education, or social work. Effective child protection is achieved by interpretation of information by every member of a core group which supports the creation of an action plan. I always remind students and experienced professionals, during our annual child protection training, that the input from each service-provider is one small part of the extensive picture which informs child protection issues. The significance of a practitioner's observation can be fully assessed only in the holistic context of other mitigating factors.

Empathy fatigue

At the beginning of my career, in the 1980s, the descriptor 'burn-out' was used to represent a weakness in professional output which related to mental and physical exhaustion of the worker. Currently, a term which can be applied is 'empathy fatigue' (Howe, 2011). Empathy fatigue is not unexpected in the context of practising within child protection; however, each professional can be supported, emotions can be managed, and anxiety can be dissipated. The professional's ability and capacity to empathise can be nurtured. Reflective practice and support/supervision should be used to highlight good effective practice in addition to areas for development. Also, colleagues should openly recognise each other's achievements on a regular informal basis. A few words of descriptive praise and verbalising actions to publicise good practice to a team can have an amazing effect upon the emotional stability and positivity of a professional in child protection.

Example from practice

Sheena is 4 years old. She presented in nursery with an unusual bruising pattern on the edge of her ear. The keyworker discussed with her room colleague and alerted the senior staff. At collection time, senior staff approached Sheena's mother: 'How are you? – Sheena has had a good morning. She ate her fruit at snack-time, and played today with a new child in the nursery.' The senior asked a question: 'I noticed that Sheena has a sore bit on her ear – what happened?' Sheena's mother responded.

Senior staff replied, 'Thanks for telling me that – it is so useful that we all share information, and you know that we always inform you if Sheena has a bump in nursery. I'll record that information about Sheena's ear in her file, as we always do, and I'll pass it on to her other workers. I appreciate you taking time to talk. Thank you, see you both tomorrow.' The incident was recorded by following child protection procedures.

The keyworker commented to the senior, 'I liked the way that you dealt with that, and I am going to take a couple of these phrases that you used because it seemed an easy and relaxed encounter with Sheena's mum although it might turn out to be child protection.' Senior staff also need positive reinforcement of good practice from room colleagues!

This incident may or may not relate to child protection, but procedures have been followed, and the parent's cooperation was welcomed. The parent-professional relationship was used to good advantage. It is important that information sharing in child protection is accurate and honest. The initial few words of greeting to Sheena's mother re-established the relationship as a medium for communication. The informal feedback from senior to parent supported this parent to listen and respond prior to the significant transfer of information in the context of potential child protection. It is essential that parents are not given explanation by staff – hence the general question. It is essential that parents do not feel culpable by questions which are promoted by staff. It is essential that parents understand that staff are following

84 *Pedagogy and the implementation gap*

procedures and not a personal agenda. Finally, it is essential that staff maintain a positive professional relationship and remind parents that nursery life will continue as usual the next day – **initial and parting comments within human interactions are valuable** and may make the difference between a parent returning to a service or not.

Supervision of the workforce is necessary so that delivery of social services adheres to policy and expectations of each organisation and maintains standards in accordance with regulations. Additionally, professionals require emotional and informational support to ensure that they have the ability, capacity, and resilience to respond to emotive challenges and to deliver an optimum service. Support and supervision are mandatory, regulated processes within a context of the social service sector; however, it is important that these strategic mechanisms are applied in response to individual needs of professionals and reflect the interpretation and resultant perception of each practitioner.

Legislation

The concept of the parent-professional relationship and the contribution to child protection has been discussed formally and informally in the context of recent legislation which is called the Children and Young People (Scotland) Act 2014 (Scottish Government, 2014). Legislation can be used to promote consistency of practice throughout a nation and to reduce the implementation gap. The rationale for this legislation was based upon a review of findings from significant cases from the last 40 years which occurred within the UK. Each inquiry into a child's death or serious injury found that effective information sharing within and between agencies was fundamental to improving the protection of children. Protection from harm includes achievement of potential which is integral to the Scottish national practice model in the context of Getting It Right for Every Child (Scottish Government, 2008).

The Children and Young People (Scotland) Act 2014 has led to a change in the approach of health visitors to supporting families with children under 5 years of age. This model, called Universal Health Visiting Pathway in Scotland Pre-birth to Pre-school, provides a framework for the creation of a therapeutic relationship, which is promoted as a medium to implement principles of good practice. These health visiting principles focus upon strengths and needs (Scottish Government, 2015). A pre-condition to applying these principles is the ability of a professional to identify the strengths of parents and to use empathic responding. The practice associated with implementation of these principles is linked to two conditions which are regular home visits and needs assessments by a health professional. The rationale of this approach

Pedagogy and the implementation gap 85

is based upon empowerment of primary carers by supporting learning and development within the parenting role in the context of a birth family culture.

Legislation and the subsequent revision of a health visiting pathway impose formal parameters upon the professional-parent relationship. The approach is designed to create a system which enables practitioners to implement support effectively and efficiently. Formalising an approach in legislation does allocate accountability and responsibility to the service-provider, and it demands a response within an allocated timeframe. The Scottish model will be researched and evaluated over the next few years. The formation and maintenance of a therapeutic relationship will continue to be dependent on the use of personal and professional skills by the practitioner (Department for Children, Schools and Families, 2010; Scottish Social Services Council, 2003).

The parent-professional relationship has particular significance in a context of child protection. It is a medium which carries bureaucracy, personal skills, and information from a professional educator to a developing person. It is a medium which directly affects the two parties involved in the relationship; however, the outcome has greatest significance for a third party – the vulnerable child. It has the potential to contribute to a system which promotes change by increasing resilience to adversity and supporting a parent's ability to make positive life choices which protect a child. The un-recordable and immeasurable aspect of this relational medium is development of a parent's self-esteem.

Professional development is continuous throughout our careers. The learning journey is solitary and interactive. It is important to recognise personal and collective achievement and to reflect upon our negative experiences as we seek knowledge and understanding. The practitioner's role, relationships, and responsibilities have been extended through research findings which led to changes in legislation, guidance, and society's expectations of the early years' worker. Relationships are key to human development, whether keyworker to child, practitioner to parent, or professional to professional. Gaining an understanding of ourselves in a childhood, parenthood, or professional role; recognising the current and potential impact that we can make upon our world; and developing resilience to adversity are the driving forces which support human beings to lead effective lives as responsible, educated, and caring citizens.

Conclusion

This book has looked at the changing role, relationships, and responsibilities of the early years' worker. The context projects accountability and demands a timely response. A relationship is an emotive connection between two people which supports development. Research indicates that

86 Pedagogy and the implementation gap

the therapeutic relationship gives optimum value for children and parents, and the principles by Rogers (1990) continue to be applicable to the twenty-first century.

As early years' practitioners, we will continue to learn and to reflect in order to protect and guide the children in our care. Research presents knowledge to professionals, and findings may relate to a specific or broad context. Theory underpins an increase in understanding, and legislation can promote consistency to the implementation of statutes in services within local authority areas and also throughout a nation. Research, legislation, generic guidance, and cultural sensitivity are features which contribute to an organisational pedagogy and serve to close the 'implementation gap.'

Key messages

- The role of the early years' worker will continue to evolve as research informs practice.
- Relationship-based practice supports development and includes keyworker to child, practitioner to parent, and professional to professional.
- Relationships formed in the earliest years provide a relational blueprint which can be used throughout a lifespan.
- Emotional wellbeing and involvement in a learning environment are increased by the support of an attachment figure.
- Pedagogy which considers cultural sensitivity in response to the needs and interests of individuals contributes to inclusion.

References

Bowlby, J. (1979). *The making and breaking of affectional bonds*. Abingdon: Routledge.
Department for Children, Schools and Families. (2009). *Common assessment framework*. Retrieved March 11, 2009, from www.dcsf.gov.uk/everychildmatters/strategy/deliveringservices1/caf/cafframework
Department for Children, Schools and Families. (2010). *The common core of skills and knowledge*. Leeds: Children's Workforce Development Council.
Howe, D. (2011). *Attachment across the life course, a brief introduction*. Basingstoke: Palgrave Macmillan.
Katz, I., La Placa, V., & Hunter, S. (2007). *Barriers to inclusion and successful engagement of parents in mainstream services*. York: Joseph Rowntree Foundation.
Lord, P., Kinder, K., Wilkin, A., Atkinson, M., & Harland, J. (2008). *Evaluating the early impact of integrated children's services*. Slough: National Foundation for Educational Research.
Scottish Government. (2008). *A guide to getting it right for every child*. Edinburgh: Scottish Government.
Scottish Government. (2012). *Common core of skills, knowledge and understanding and values for the 'children's workforce' in Scotland*. Edinburgh: Scottish Government.

Scottish Government. (2014). *Children and young people (Scotland) Act. (2014).* Edinburgh: Scottish Government.
Scottish Government. (2015). *Universal health visiting pathway in Scotland, pre-birth to pre-school.* Edinburgh: Scottish Government.
Scottish Social Services Council. (2003). *Codes of practice for social services workers and employers, code 1.* Dundee: Scottish Social Services Council.
Whitters, H. G. (2015). *Perceptions of the influences upon the parent-professional relationship in a context of early intervention and child protection.* Published doctoral thesis. Retrieved January 2016, from http://ethos.bl.uk/OrderDetails.do?uin=uk.bl.ethos.655502
Whitters, H. G. (2016). *The parent-professional relationship in child protection.* Retrieved April 2016, from withscotland.org/download/the-parent-professional-relationship-in-child-protection

Index

ambivalent attachment 36–9
attachment: ambivalent 38–9; avoidant 39–41; chaotic 41–3; insecure 25, 52; secure 13, 15, 17, 19, 25, 27, 31, 35, 52; theory 8, 12, 14–16, 25–6, 29–31, 33
autism 38
autobiographical self 35, 43–5
avoidant attachment 39–41

basic-level learning 60
Bio-Ecological Systems of Human Development 52
bureaucracy 59–60

California Adverse Childhood Experience Study 33
case studies 75
chaotic attachment 41–3
child development: of the autobiographical self 35; perceptions 65; relationships and 32; theory 7–8, 12, 14–16, 26–7, 29–31
child involvement 10–11
child protection: bureaucracy 59–60; demand characteristics 63; in early years 49–68; expressed need 61; felt need 60–1; informal verbal communication 61–2; negative perception of 66–7; normative need 61; optimal communication 62–3; pedagogy and 78–9; peripheral participation 63–4; personality influence 67–8; policy 52–3; positive perception of 65–6;

power within relationship 56–9; practitioner's perspective 53; relationship-based practice 53–4; society's perspective 53; theory 49–51
Children and Young People (Scotland) Act 2014 84
chill-out zones 19
coherent narrative 15
communication: informal verbal 61–2; optimal 62–3
connectors 62
convergence 65, 80
cultural consonance 62
cultural sensitivity 75
curriculum 8–9

deep-level learning 31, 60
demand characteristics 63
dependency theory 31–2
divergence 65, 79

Ecological Systems of Human Development 51–2
Effective Provision of Pre-school Education 12
Effective Provision of Pre-school Education Project 32
emotional care 7–8
empathy 46
empathy fatigue 82–4
expressed need 61

Family-Nurse Partnership 54
felt need 60–1

90 Index

guidance 75

heuristic play 12–17
High-Scope programme 8

informal verbal communication 61–2
inner working model 74
insecure attachment 25, 38, 52
interpretation 57, 60

kangaroo-care 28
knowledge 74

learning 31, 57, 60, 65, 76
legislation 84–5
Leuven Involvement Scale 10

macro-system 51
meso-system 51, 63
micro-systems 51–2, 63, 65
mind mindedness 34
mind, theory of 45–6
multi-disciplinary teams 75–6
multiple micro-systems 51
My World Triangle 81

National Parenting Strategy for Scotland 2012 53
National Practice Models 8, 81
normative need 61
nursery nurses 7–9
nurture classes 18–19
nurture corners 18–19
nurture rooms 18–19
nurturing 18–19

operational perspective 57

parents 76
pedagogy: child protection and 78–9; implementation gap 78, 86; planning 76–8
peers 75–6
perceptions: of child protection 65–7; convergence of 80; differences of 64–5; divergence of 79–80
peripheral participation 63–4
personality 67–8
physical contact 16
planning 76–8

play: concept of 9–10; creation and implementation of environment 76–8; heuristic 12–13; therapeutic 17, 18; treasure basket 12–13
Plowden Report 8
policy 75
positive stress 27
power 56–9
practice examples: ambivalent attachment 36–7; attachment theory 29–31; avoidant attachment 39; bureaucracy 59; chaotic attachment 41–2; development of autobiographical sense of self 43–5; empathy fatigue 83; expressed need 61; felt need 60–1; negative perception of child protection 66–7; perceptions 64–5, 81–2; peripheral participation 64; personality influence 66–7; positive perception of child protection 65–6; power within relationship 57–8; professional learners 42–3; stress 27–8
practice models 8–9, 20–1
professional development 85
professionalism 20

quality-assurance system 56

reflection 44
reflective practice 73–4, 83
Reggio Emilia approach 8
relationship-based practice 53–4
relationships: attachment theory 29–31; avoidant attachment 39–41; bureaucracy 59–60; in childhood and adulthood 32–3; dependency theory 31–2; development and 32; development of autobiographical sense of self 43–5; earliest 25–6; personality influence 67–8; power within 56–9; purpose of 34; quality-assurance system 56; relationship-based practice 53–4; stress 26–9; therapeutic 55–6, 85; understanding of self 38–9; value of 56
relationship therapy 17
resilience 17–18, 42
Resilience Matrix 81

restorative experience 19
role-modelling 39–41

scenarios 75
schemas 15–16
secure attachment 13, 15, 17, 19, 25, 27, 31, 35, 52
selective mutism 18
selfdeveloping autobiographical sense of 43–5; development of autobiographical sense of self 35; false sense of 40–1; understanding of 38–9
self-esteem 45
Shanarri Wellbeing wheel 81
Social-Address Model 63
social collective function 62
socially orientated beliefs 57

social referencing 75
stress 26–9
sympathy 46

theory 75
therapeutic play 17, 18
therapeutic relationship: aspects 55; formation and maintenance of 85; outcome 56; purpose of 55
tolerable stress 27
treasure basket 13–14

Universal Health Visiting Pathway Scotland: Pre-Birth to Pre-School model 84–5

wellbeing: child 11–21; emotional 9–10, 16; role of environment on 28

Taylor & Francis eBooks

Helping you to choose the right eBooks for your Library

Add Routledge titles to your library's digital collection today. Taylor and Francis ebooks contains over 50,000 titles in the Humanities, Social Sciences, Behavioural Sciences, Built Environment and Law.

Choose from a range of subject packages or create your own!

Benefits for you
- Free MARC records
- COUNTER-compliant usage statistics
- Flexible purchase and pricing options
- All titles DRM-free.

REQUEST YOUR FREE INSTITUTIONAL TRIAL TODAY

Free Trials Available
We offer free trials to qualifying academic, corporate and government customers.

Benefits for your user
- Off-site, anytime access via Athens or referring URL
- Print or copy pages or chapters
- Full content search
- Bookmark, highlight and annotate text
- Access to thousands of pages of quality research at the click of a button.

eCollections – Choose from over 30 subject eCollections, including:

Archaeology	Language Learning
Architecture	Law
Asian Studies	Literature
Business & Management	Media & Communication
Classical Studies	Middle East Studies
Construction	Music
Creative & Media Arts	Philosophy
Criminology & Criminal Justice	Planning
Economics	Politics
Education	Psychology & Mental Health
Energy	Religion
Engineering	Security
English Language & Linguistics	Social Work
Environment & Sustainability	Sociology
Geography	Sport
Health Studies	Theatre & Performance
History	Tourism, Hospitality & Events

For more information, pricing enquiries or to order a free trial, please contact your local sales team:
www.tandfebooks.com/page/sales

The home of Routledge books

www.tandfebooks.com